# J. R. BOOTH:

Lumberman, Railroad Builder, Industrialist and Great Canadian

*Roderick MacKay*

Published by FastPencil

Published by FastPencil
307 Orchard City Drive
Suite 210
Campbell CA 95008 USA
info@fastpencil.com
(408) 540-7571
(408) 540-7572 (Fax)
http://www.fastpencil.com

Cover layout by Capitola Design (www.capitoladesign.com). Front cover Image provided by Library and Archives Canada PA-028000. Back cover image provided by Library and Archives Canada A00399

Printed in the United States of America.

First Edition

*I particularly thank Sandra Barr, my dear wife, for her patience and encouragement while I worked on this seemingly endless task.*

⁊❧

# *Acknowledgments*

This effort derives in considerable part from the excellent work of Clarence Coons, and John Trinnell, each of whom produced informative booklets or books on Booth. Unfortunately, those excellent publications are no longer easily accessible to the public. It was that condition, and a continuing interest in J.R. Booth by clients of The Friends of Algonquin Park bookstores, that prompted the writing of this book. Dan Strickland encouraged my early efforts to write about the great man by publishing "The Stuff of Legends" in the Algonquin Park newsletter "The Raven". Fellow Park historian Gaye Clemson and I decided to partner in producing titles independently for a "More About...." series of histories of Algonquin Park, a project in which she has been the more prolific. Gaye was very patient, encouraging and supportive in helping me with the self-publishing learning curve. I am grateful.

Thanks are extended to the Algonquin Park Museum Archives, Queen's University Archives, The Library and Archives of Canada, the Ontario Archives, Paul Mackey and Joan Barclay Drummond for permission to reproduce photographs from their collections.

Tom Ballantine provided some valuable fact finding and assisted with comment. Ron Tozer and Niall MacKay provided valuable assistance and comment. Morag Coyne came to my rescue in finding and copying some information in long-sought-for microfilms at Queen's University.

After 34 years, Niall MacKay is no longer the only Booth author in the family.

Roderick (Rory) MacKay
Lake of Two Rivers, Algonquin Park

# Contents

# An Ottawa Valley Legend

*John Rudolphus Booth, in his later years, standing beside a load of timber in 1924. Library and Archives Canada C-046480*

IN FUR HAT, LEATHER gloves, and wrapped in a thick woolen coat buttoned up against the frosty air of Ottawa, he stood next to the flatcar of huge squared pine logs recently cut in the Shirley Lake district of Algonquin Park. Now needing a cane for physical support, but fully in control of his intellectual faculties at ninety-seven years of age, J.R. Booth observed a trainload of square timber as it passed through the city on a bright December day in 1924.

The story of John Rudophus Booth is one of a lumberman, an industrialist, a self-made millionaire, the owner of probably the largest company owned by one man in his day, and a great Canadian.

2 • Roderick MacKay

Here and there within the Ottawa Valley, Booth's name lives on in the landscape. There is a Chemin Booth in Chelsea, Quebec, and a Booth Street in Ottawa. There was a "Booth building" at 165 Sparks Street, Ottawa, and there is a large Booth family monument in Ottawa's Beechwood Cemetery, Canada's National Cemetery. Between Huntsville and Parry Sound, one can find a J.R. Booth section of the Seguin Snowmobile Trail. In Algonquin Provincial Park, Booth's name is associated with the self-guided Booth's Rock Trail adjacent to Rock Lake, Booth Lake on the Opeongo River and, nearby, the old Booth depot farm on which there is said to be a large rock dubbed "J.R. Booth's armchair." His name also comes up associated with the Park's Old Railway Bike Trail, and the Track and Tower Trail. Those geographic legacies are due, in part, to the long-term influence this man had on the landscapes of the Ottawa Valley. In fact it is nearly impossible to relate the history of the Ottawa Valley without some reference to J.R. Booth, and that certainly applies to the Algonquin Park area.

Much of Algonquin Park was at one time licensed to J.R. Booth for logging, even after it became a Park in 1893. The Park was set aside as much as a timber reserve as it was set aside as a wildlife sanctuary and playground for vacationers. Although the timber rights were leased from the Ontario government, rather than the land being sold outright, those limits were very much Booth's domain. It was from those forests that he derived much of his great wealth. It was Booth's railway through the southern section of Algonquin Park that led to the cutting of all tree species in the Park, not just the easily floated red and white pine. It was that same railway — for a time one of the busiest routes in Canada — that helped to open up Algonquin Park to tourism *and for this reason alone, it had an incalcuable influence on the development and history of Algonquin*" (Strickland, 1993).

John Rudolphus Booth was a giant in the lumber trade for such a long time that throughout the Twentieth Century just about everyone around the Ottawa Valley or Algonquin Park had worked for him, or claimed to have worked for him, or had met him, or had heard of him. He was often referred to as "The Great John R." (Coons 1978). Despite that fame and familiarity, fully fifty years after his death there were no books written about the man or his enterprises.

A brief article, "The Stuff of Legends", published in the Algonquin Park newsletter *The Raven* in 1975 (Strickland 1993), was one of but a few to recognize in print the life and times of this great man since the wide newspaper coverage of his death in December 1925. Now, in the first decades of the Twenty-first Century, with most of the few books about him currently out of print, people still want to know about the man of humble beginnings who became a giant of Canadian industry.

At the time of his death it was noted that *"a sort of legendary halo had been woven around the name of J.R. Booth"* (Anonymous 1925j). While the information in this volume is primarily factual, it would not do full service to the man to exclude some of the stories which contributed to the legend. The author is indebted to those authors who wrote earlier works about J.R. Booth, thus paving the way for this small volume. Not intended to be an exhaustive biography of Booth, one could suggest that this is just enough **"more about...."** him.

*J.R. Booth (r) and unknown man. Note the pulpwood and rolls of newsprint. Library and Archives Canada, PA-042562*

# J. R. Booth: The Early Years

*The waters of the Chaudiere Falls powered the sawmills and gristmills in the industrial heart of Bytown and Hull. Library and Archives Canada PA-012497, detail*

JOHN RUDOLPHUS BOOTH WAS born to John Booth and Helen Rowley Booth on April 5th, 1827, in the "eastern townships" of Quebec, near the village of Waterloo. Most descriptions of Booth's childhood suggest that his formal schooling was rudimentary, the usual situation for a farm boy at the time. Booth's real education, throughout his life, was what today would be termed experiential. He learned how to operate machinery on the family farm. According to some sources, Booth was interested in the mechanics of water-powered mills from an early age, even constructing working models on streams near his childhood home (Coons 1978).

As a teenager he left home and found a position as a carpenter's helper in New York State. Then he had an opportunity to go west to join the California gold rush. A letter home to that effect prompted his father to seek him out and bring him home again to the farm. Still eager to find his own way in the world, at age 21 he began working for the Central Vermont Railroad as a carpenter, building bridges. Three years later, finding he was not getting ahead financially, John Booth returned to Canada. In January 1853, he married Rosalinda (Benidickson 2000, Trinnell 1998) or Roselinda (Coons 1978, French 1963) Cook, the daughter of a neighbouring farmer. He continued to work as a carpenter in the Waterloo area for a while.

## Making a Reputation

In or about 1852 (French 1963) or 1854 according to some authors (Trinnell 1998), and post-1857 according to others, Booth and his wife and his new daughter took a stage coach to Montreal and then a steamer up-river to Bytown (now Ottawa). The population of Bytown was about 8,000 people at that time. The exact nature of his employment during those early years in Bytown is uncertain. According to some sources his first employment was across the river in a machine shop in Hull (Coons 1978). Other sources suggest he had a contract to assist a Mr. Reid in constructing a mill in Sherbrooke, Quebec and then with Reid doing similar work for Andrew Leamy, in Hull. It is known he worked for Leamy (Anonymous 1925j).

As the story goes, Booth arrived in Bytown with just nine dollars in his pocket. While the same humble beginning (and financial resource) has been claimed of others, and the value of nine dollars then was much more than nine dollars today, there is little doubt that Booth had very little in the way of financial resources at first. Housing was difficult to find in Hull, so Booth rented three rooms in the home of William Fotheringham on Queen Street, from which he walked the three miles distance to his work (Trinnell 1998).

Apparently, such was his determination to improve his lot in life, in the evenings he and his wife split cedar logs into roof shingles to sell (French 1963). Cedar logs would be sawn by hand to short lengths and a froe and mallet would be used to split off the "shakes." A draw knife would be used to do the thinning and shaping. Such industry at the end of his regular work day fits in with what we know of the hard-working character of the man. When he had enough shingles made, he would carry them to a place where he could sell them, and then with the proceeds buy groceries from local merchants. According to the *Ottawa Journal*:

*"On one occasion Mr. Booth was short of money – in fact had only enough ready cash to pay for half a load of feed – but the grist mill owner knew his man and insisted that he take a full load. Mr. Booth reluctantly consented and started for home, but after a lapse of some hours he returned to the grist mill and told the proprietor that it had always been a fixed rate with him never to run in debt, and insisted that the miller take back such a part of the load as he could not pay cash for. Strict adherence to the policy of keeping out of debt was one of the factors that contributed to the foundations of the Booth fortune"* (Anonymous 1925j).

It must be said that Booth made his move to Ottawa with fortunate timing, because the British and American governments had negotiated a free trade deal between the British North American colonies and the United States, which came into effect in 1854. That Reciprocity Treaty opened up American markets to Canadian lumber. It was through the twelve years of the treaty that Booth was able to develop a sawmill and lumbering empire, with its focus at the Ottawa River's Chaudiere Falls. Most of the great figures in the square timber trade had been British, but the lumber trade which rose after 1850 in the thriving sawmill town on the Ottawa River was dominated by industrialists from the United States. Booth, however, was eventually engaged in both of these aspects of the forest industry, and, as we know, he was born in British North America, now Canada.

After working on the construction of Andrew Leamy's steam-driven sawmill on Leamy Lake, on the Lower Canada side of the Ottawa River, Booth was hired as manager of the mill. No doubt that was partly because of his inside knowledge of the mill's workings. He held that position for a year. Then, apparently, for eight months Booth operated his own machine shop until it was destroyed by fire (Coons 1978).

Recovering from that disaster, he rented an empty gristmill from Alonzo Wright, installed two shingle-making machines, and began producing cedar shingles in quantity (Coons 1978). A year later, when Wright doubled the rent, Booth refused to pay the increase. Instead he secured a ten year lease on an unused water-driven sawmill, formerly operated by

Phillip Thompson on the Ontario side of the Chaudiere Falls, The sawmill was small, but it contained 27 upright saws and a circular saw (Hugheson and Bond 1987), enough to produce laths and lumber if one had a market for it. It was 1858, and there was a good market. The Chaudiere Falls had been a major obstacle for the rafts of square timber making their way from the headwaters of the Algonquin dome to Quebec City, for shipment across the Atlantic. Now dammed, water from above the falls was fed to water wheels - which turned the gears - which ran the saws - that cut the pine – and made the lumber, stacked so tall – that became the economic foundation of pioneer Ottawa.

John Booth was not alone at the Chaudiere Falls. The firm of Bronson and Weston had set up sawmills there in 1853, soon to be followed by Ezra Butler Eddy, A.H. Baldwin, Levi Young, and the firm of Perley and Pattee, all Americans. Booth would eventually surpass them all.

### His First Big Break
Ottawa, which had been known as Bytown until 1855, was chosen by Queen Victoria to be the capital of the united Province of Canada. A structure was required for the house of Parliament, and the contract to supply the wood for the roof and elsewhere in the building was advertised in 1859. Booth provided the lowest bid, and won the contract. Booth obtained the wood for what became Canada's Parliament buildings in 1867, just a short distance upriver from his mills. Some of the pine Booth provided can still be seen in Canada's Parliamentary Library. Standing behind the Centre Block, it was the only part to survive a great fire in 1916 which destroyed the original Centre Block of the Parliament buildings.

It was around that time that parts of the Booth legend began. It is said that, on that job, Booth was the first to use horses in the logging trade, supposedly when finding ways to cut costs (Coons 1978). But that is indeed a myth. While it is true that many early timbermakers used oxen to haul the heavy square timbers to the water's edge, the Wrights of Hull were using horses in their camps in the 1830s, and the McLachlin Brothers had followed suit by the 1840s (Lee 2006).

The Parliament buildings contract, and a brief but profitable partnership with another lumberman, A.W. Soper, provided Booth with sufficient funds to purchase the Thompson mill outright in 1860. He was also able to purchase Lyman Perkins' neighbouring mill lots as well (Benidickson 2000). The American Civil War caused a slump in trade with the United States, but by 1867 business had picked up again and Booth had opened a distribution centre for his lumber at Rouses Point on Lake Champlain.

It is said that, throughout his life, Booth's best collateral when seeking financial backing was the presence of calluses on his hands, demonstrating an ability to work hard (Gard 1904). He had also established a firm business reputation in Ottawa. But now more wood was needed to supply his sawmills.

*Pre-1916 Centre Block of Canada's Parliament buildings for which Booth supplied the wood. Library and Archives Canada PA-02322*

*Ottawa's Parliamentary Library, the only part that survived a 1916 fire. Library and Archives Canada PA-023214*

# J. R. Booth: The Lumberman

*Much of Booth's fortune was made from pines logged on his limits on the Madawaska River. Library and Archives Canada PA-120333, detail*

NOT ONLY WAS J.R. Booth making lumber, now he was also making money. Throughout his life, Booth was known to have the courage to take financial risk if it led to eventual gain. That was soon demonstrated in his acquisition of timber limits; vast tracts of land in the hinterlands on which the "leasee" could cut the timber (the land was not owned so the title remained with the Crown). The purchase of a good lease could lead to riches.

### The Egan Estate Limit

One of the most important gambles of Booth's life was the purchase of what was known as the Egan Estate timber limit on the Madawaska River, in 1867. In this case the term "estate" referred to John Egan's holdings at the time of his death, not a large mansion with well-kept grounds. Encompassing a section of the Madawaska River, much of it within modern-day Algonquin Park, this large block of prime pine had been held by the timber-maker John Egan until his death in 1857, and thereafter for ten years by his trustees. Much of the biggest pine on the limit had been cut for square timber, but there was still plenty of large pine left for sawlogs. John Booth's cousin, Robert Booth, had checked the Egan limits for marketable trees. According to one source he reported back that *"The pine stands like grass for number and for quality they are unexcelled"* (Gard 1904). It was expected that the price for the limit would be fairly high. Booth was backed by the Bank of North America, which apparently was willing to lend him whatever monies were required to make the purchase. According to published reports, the purchase unfolded dramatically. The auction had attracted many of the biggest names in the lumber industry, as the former Egan limits held some of the largest stands of uncut pine in the Ottawa Valley. It was thought by some that the limits could be purchased for twenty to twenty-five thousand dollars. J.R. Booth stood with his bank manager. Dressed as a labourer, some may not have noticed that he continued to bid well beyond the expected price. It is unknown what agreement there was with the bank, but it is known that Booth's cousin had told him to buy at any price. It was felt by many of the lumbermen present that Booth had been most foolhardy by submitting the winning bid of $45,000 (Coons 1978). Booth said:

*"When this tract was put up for sale about fifty-one years ago, after the death of Mr. John Egan, its former owner, I told the auctioneer that no matter what bid was made the last bid was to be mine. I raised no voice. With bidding in the vicinity of $35,000 someone said the price was too high, but finally I paid $10,000 more and bought the limit. Afterwards the very man who had said the price was too high when the bidding was about $35,000 offered me $10,000 more than my bargain. A friend of mine in Ottawa advised me strongly not to refuse the $10,000, a clear gain, but I told him that I knew enough not to take $100,000 for the limit"* (Anonymous 1906).

In a rare interview in 1906, Booth reflected on the lasting value of the Madawaska limit, which he continued to log to that date: *"A season's take had never amounted to less than 150,000 logs and sometimes had gone up to 300,000. The Egan limits on the Madawaska were the basis of all my fortune"* (Trinnell 1998).

Booth continued to buy up timber limits, particularly during a depression from 1874 to 1876 when prices fell. Soon he had limits on the Ottawa, Petawawa, Bonnechere, Madawaska, Opeongo, Mattawa and Montreal rivers, as well as the Noire, Coulonge and Dumoine in Quebec. Booth's strategy for buying was to determine a price he was willing to pay, and wait for others to bid close to that value. Then he would begin to bid aggressively, frightening off most of his competition (Stevenson nd).

### Booth and the Square Timber Trade

Although best known for his large sawmills, Booth's men cut square timber as well as sawlogs. Some of his timber rafts were among the largest on the Ottawa River. The process of making square timber is well known to some, but bears repeating. Large pine were selected and cut down by axe. Cross-cut saws were not used for that purpose, even after 1870 when they were used for cutting sawlogs. The logs were squared, using broad-axes that were flat on one side and with a bevel on the other. Only logs with straight grain and relatively free of knots were squared completely. Logs with inferior wood were abandoned "as felled" or partially completed.

After being cut and squared by axe in the woods, the timbers were hauled to waterways and driven as individual "sticks" down the tributaries to the Ottawa River with the spring flood. Once they reached the exit of each tributary at the Ottawa River the individual sticks were made into cribs about 26 feet wide and as long as the individual sticks, say fifty feet. Many cribs would be joined together to form a large timber raft. The raft would drift downstream with the current, assisted as necessary by sails, or the large oar-like sweeps manned by the raft's crew. The men lived and slept right on the raft, their meals prepared over an open fire under a crude roof. The fire was built on sand, contained by wooden beams and laid on the surface of the raft.

By 1840, timbers could be rafted from as far up-river as Lake Timiskaming. Rapids at des Joachim and at Lac des Chats required a means of avoiding the obstacles. Each raft would be disassembled to allow passage of its constituent cribs through inclined slides slightly wider than the cribs. A timber slide to by-pass the Chaudiere Falls at Ottawa had been constructed in 1828. Once re-assembled below Parliament Hill, the rafts drifted downstream or were towed by steam boats to reach the Port of Quebec where the timbers were sold for overseas export and then loaded on sailing ships bound for England.

The main river was not the only waterway needing by-passes around falls, and other means had to be devised to enable a smooth passage of logs downstream. Chutes that would take a single stick were constructed; dams controlled water flow; rocks were blasted to open or widen channels; and booms and piers were built to improve the flow of logs. On some streams those river "improvements" were paid for by private means, but on others the work was done collectively or by government. The Upper Ottawa Improvement Company was formed in 1866 for making improvements to driving the Ottawa River, with Booth as one of the founders (Hugheson and Bond 1987). Later, in 1888, he became the founding president of the Madawaska Improvement Company Limited (Benidickson 2000).

### Booth and the Cockburn Pointer

During the river-drive it was necessary to carry both men and supplies downstream in boats. Canoes may have served this purpose originally, but the wear and tear of the drive required a vessel of greater durability. One specific type of drive boat, the Pointer, was manufactured by John Cockburn, an English boat builder. He and his brother David had bid on a woodworking contract to make the carved ends for the seats on which the elected representatives would sit in the new Parliament Buildings in Ottawa. Having secured the contract, the brothers emigrated to Upper Canada. Legend has it that the long, narrow design of the Pointer drive boat, with its rounded V-bottom and high pointed ends, was influenced by J.R. Booth. Such involvement in detail was typical of Booth's approach to the work in the woods, for it was said *"He knew the forest as a sailor knows the sea"* (Roberts 1934). It is possible that Booth met Cockburn and discussed drive boats while fulfilling their various contracts on the Parliament buildings. The first Pointers were made in Ottawa under contract to Booth and shipped to the woods near Pembroke. There is no doubt that Booth would have purchased many of those boats for his far-flung operations. Demand by other companies in need of the same kind of boat and the expansion of the timber and lumber trades upstream prompted a move to Pembroke in 1865, where the Cockburn firm continued to produce Pointers for the lumbering trade until 1969 (Lee-whiting 1970).

By 1872, Booth had built an empire. He realized *"that if his Chaudiere undertakings were to survive he must ensure that his timber holdings were extensive enough to provide the large quantities of logs required by his mills"* (Coons 1978). He was still cutting both square timber and sawlogs on his limits. His sawmills were producing between 26 and 30 million board feet of sawn lumber from the hundreds of thousands of logs cut annually. The lumber was dried in stacks on a piling yard that covered over 10 acres of land in what is now downtown Ottawa. When dried, the lumber was loaded into barges for the trip down the Ottawa River; some barges followed the St. Lawrence River to markets in eastern Canada, and others used the Chambly, Champlain, and Erie canal route to markets in the United States.

As required by the Act Respecting the Marking of Timber of 1870, Booth registered marks in 1873 to distinguish his logs from others being driven down the Ottawa and its tributaries. The earliest of Booth's timber stamps, and the one seen most frequently on dead-head logs in Algonquin Park's rivers, was a diamond shape or equal-sided parallelogram in which was placed a JB combined. The timber mark would be impressed in the ends of logs with an embossed stamping hammer. Booth's bark mark, cut on the side of a log with an axe, was an oval with four "legs" representing a turtle as seen from above. The ease with which this mark could be cut was likely the reason for its selection as Booth's bark mark.

### A Visit To One of Booth's Limits

Booth continued to expand his interests in Canada, capitalizing on the depression years between 1874 and 1876 to buy up additional timber limits. His limits spanned the Ottawa Valley and even beyond. From Robert Phipps, Clerk of Forestry for the Ontario government, we get a glimpse of some of Booth's forest holdings in 1884:

*"The next point in our journey is Callendar, one of the headquarters of Booth and Co.'s large lumbering establishment, where we are hospitably received by Mr. Mark Cahill, acting at Callendar for Mr. Booth....In travelling the next day with Mr. Cahill, he pointed out from the summit of a hill, overlooking a large lake, a great and almost untouched forest, mostly of pine. The scene was grand. ...here we view that sight beyond others magnificent, the waving crests where far extend right, left, and centre to the extreme and distant horizon the dark green billows of the great Canadian pine an ocean*

*of verdure.... It is most beautiful, and might remain so. Yet it needs but a match, a careless hunter, a settler pressed by want and anxious to grow what wheat the scanty soil will yield, and this vast extent of millions of dollars worth of pine — its possibilities of growing millions more — shall be a blackened wilderness of worthless trunks, scattered above a soil burnt into a barrenness well-nigh utter. Part of this was in Mr. Booth's limit — part is Government land. It is a wood the forester would love to keep a wood"* (Phipps 1885).

Phipps went on to examine the condition in which the loggers left the woods:

*"In the evening of the same day, examining the state in which a bush was left after most of the logs had been removed, being taken, in this case, both for square timber and logs, we found that the surface was thickly spread, here and there where trees had been squared, with pine chips of all sizes, and close by, scattered in confusion, the heads of the trees, with others, which had been felled to assist in the operation. Undoubtedly, there was much more lying rubbish than elsewhere. But Mr. Cahill was of the opinion that the chips on the ground soon grew damp, and would not catch fire from sparks, though a fire once started, they would give it much more material. On being asked whether, if the limbs were chopped off the tree heads after each tree was cut down, so as to form a dense pile on the ground, it would not be safer, he doubted it, as even then the top would be dry. It was, as he said, noticeable that rubbish abounded everywhere — dead branches in heaps, dry combustibles on the ground in all directions, which was ready to catch and carry fire, even in places where no timber had been got out. To clean up after the lumbermen would be, he said, a great expense, and yet much would be left"* (Phipps 1885).

### Booth's Sawlog Empire

Describing Booth's empire in 1893, the same year as the establishment of Algonquin Park, would use up a barrel-full of superlatives. There were 4,000 men employed in his lumber camps, and over 4,000 square miles of timber limits. The *American Lumberman* described the extent of those limits as: *"sufficient timber land to make a strip a mile wide reaching across Canada from the Atlantic to the Pacific"* (Anonymous 1904). In Ottawa, the 1,500 men in his mills produced 100,000,000 to 115,000,000 board feet of lumber a year or about 20% of the production of all the mills in the Ottawa Valley (Coons 1978). Had there been a Guinness Book of Records in 1896, and a category for lumbering operations, Booth would have easily been the champion of the world. None of his Ottawa competitors were producing half of the lumber his mills were sawing (Benidickson 2000).

Despite the overall growth of his empire, Booth was familiar with adversity. Fire was always Booth's great business challenge. In 1893, Booth's mill and piling yards were destroyed by fire. Booth rebuilt. He also bought up the Perley and Pattee sawmills adjacent to his burned mill and added improved machinery. Then, in 1895, his planing mill and piling yards in Burlington, Vermont, burned. Booth rebuilt, turning down a substantial financial inducement offered by the Burlington town council.

His Ottawa mills were burned out again in 1900 and 1903. *"Booth's energetic leadership and the hard work of his employees, aided by a powerful water system that he had installed after a fire in 1894 and the fact that the buildings were somewhat out of the direct line of the fire, which jumped the river where the channel was narrowest, saved his sawmills. However, he lost over 55 million board feet of lumber"* (Hugheson and Bond 1987). Each time he was burned out, Booth rebuilt; bigger and better.

Booth faced similar challenges with fire in the woods. A large fire started in the Madawaska River watershed, near Whitney. Apparently there was little concern about much of the twenty-five square miles of forest burned, until Booth's prized limits near Madawaska were threatened. Thanks to the efforts of fire rangers and men from Booth's railway, both the timber limits and the town of Madawaska were spared from the flames (Anonymous 1902b).

In 1925 it was reported: *"In the summer months, the saw mills are kept running day and night, and about 2,000 men are employed in and around the mills seven months in the year. During the winter months an army of between 3,000 and 4,000 men, with hundreds of teams of horses, is engaged in the woods getting the supply of logs for the coming season's cut. The thousands upon thousands of logs that are cut up into timber, deals, lathes, shingles or used in the manufacture of pulp, are obtained from the Booth limits in the Madawaska district and along the tributaries of the Ottawa River on both the Ontario and Quebec sides. These limits cover the immense area of approximately 7,000 square miles of which 129 square miles are in the Madawaska district"* (Anonymous 1925j).

J.R. Booth, many times over a millionaire, was often referred to as a timber baron. From Booth's perspective that was an altogether inappropriate term, as a baron has a hereditary title and Booth considered himself every inch a self-made man. Just a few years before his death he commented on the means by which he obtained his fortunes: *"People seem to think that the successful business man that they call a "baron" has had his wealth wished upon him. They think he came into easy money by a government favour. I never secured an acre of timber from any government except in open competition and, as the highest bidder, I paid the maximum price for it and any other man could have had it if he were willing to pay more; favouritism played no part whatsoever"* (Coons 1978).

Of course Booth's empire had been built on pine, but previously he and others had lobbied for permission to cut other tree species within Algonquin Park, including cedar, hemlock, tamarack, black birch, yellow birch and black ash (Anonymous 1900). The Algonquin Park Act of 1900 established that in law. In 1912, Booth relinquished his right to cut black and yellow birch, replacing those species with balsam fir (Anonymous 1912), possibly to provide a source of wood for his pulp mills.

In 1908, J.R. Booth was the owner of the last raft of square timber to travel down the Ottawa River (Trinnell 1998). Booth issued permits to Ottawa residents who wished to experience the last ride of a crib down the slides, a nostalgic re-enactment in celebration of the three hundredth anniversary of the City of Quebec (Hugheson and Bond 1987).

Although John Booth's years were advancing, he was very much still a "hands-on" businessman. A September 1913 fire caused $100,000 damage to a Booth mill. Booth went down to the mill to help. His presence was a great asset to the firemen because he knew the layout of his mill so well. Rather than let his men be idle, and slow production even more, about 1100 of 1500 men out of work as result of fire were reassigned to other jobs a few days later and were kept working on Booth's instructions.

J.R. Booth continued to be much interested in his Egan Estate timber limit near Madawaska, travelling to it each autumn by rail in his private railway car. Although the Ottawa timber-men are often accused by historians of having wastefully "clear-cut" their limits, the longevity of this particular limit speaks otherwise, as it continued to provide pine for over sixty years of Booth's lifetime, usually at a rate of 150,000 to 300,000 logs per year. When his company took out a special rail shipment of square timber for the British Admiralty in 1924, the pines on the limit were described as ranging from *"250 to 500 years old, up to 175 feet in height, and ... clear of branches for 100 feet."* Of the sticks on the ninety-eight flatcars, the timber with the greatest volume of wood from this cut was 36 inches square and 36 feet long (Anonymous 1925a).

Lumbering and mill work over all those early years required much horsepower, on the hoof, so Booth had to become a farm owner as well as a mill owner. Not only did he have depot farms scattered among his lumber camps to provide local pasturage, such as those at Kioshkokwi Lake, Booth Lake and Grand Lake in Algonquin Park, he also had farms near Ottawa. According to one newspaper:

*"Mr. J.R. Booth was one of the largest farm owners in this district and the country in the vicinity of Hull and Ottawa has benefited greatly as a result. Old timers now remember when the beautiful site now the Dominion Experimental Farm was part of the Booth Farm, and when Mr. Booth sold this tract to the Federal Government"* (Anonymous 1925j).

In more ways than this was J.R. Booth an example of diversification of business interests.

C-075265

*Squaring a timber at Aylen Lake, about 1895. Library and Archives Canada C-075265, detail*

*A pointer boat in rapids. Algonquin Park Museum Archives 1104*

*The cookery or camboose on a raft, surrounded by small dwellings. Library and Archives Canada PA-008405*

*Timber raft from the Madawaska limits. Library and Archives Canada PA-011370*

*Top: Barges carried Booth's lumber to both domestic and American Markets. Library and Archives Canada PA-012501 Bottom: A Booth raft. Library and Archives Canada C-0006096*

C-000020

*Perley and Pattee mill at Ottawa purchased by Booth. Library and Archives Canada C-00020 (Top -detail left, Bottom -detail right)*

*Top: Booth stamp hammer and the mark it made on a log. Bottom: J.R. Booth's Turtle bark mark easily made with an axe.*

# J. R Booth: The Railroad Builder

*Booth at age 54. Library and Archives Canada PA-25545 detail*

EVER SINCE HE GOT into the business of cutting lumber, the seasonal freeze-up of the waterways hampered both the supply of wood to Booth's mills and the shipment of sawn lumber to market. This set Booth to looking for a cost-effective solution. Since the mid-Nineteenth Century was a time when railways were all the rage, Booth got thinking along those lines.

Plans had been afoot since 1871 to build a north-south railway to join Ottawa with the United States. Charters had been taken out for two railways, north and south of the St Lawrence River, to be joined by a bridge. Due to financial hardships, after seven years not a rail had been laid. Booth agreed to help out financially, but soon found that unless he wished to risk all his investment he was best to take a more hands-on approach.

### The Canada Atlantic Railway

J. R. Booth and fellow lumberman William G. Perley, both of Ottawa, combined forces with J. Gregory Smith, later Governor of Vermont, in buying up the majority of stock for those failing railway projects, and began to promote what was to be known as The Canada Atlantic Railway (Bell 1991). The Canadian-built line would connect with the Central Vermont Railway. Of course the idea was to provide a means of transporting Booth's and Perley's lumber south throughout the year, without the seasonal delays caused by the winter freeze-up of the canals. In exchange it was hoped that anthracite coal for home heating and industrial purposes could be shipped north to eastern Ontario and Ottawa. There would be business for the railway in both directions. In addition, it is believed Booth did not want to depend on the Canadian Pacific Railway for shipment of freight from Renfrew to Ottawa (MacKay 1981).

The first rails were laid on the north shore of the St. Lawrence River in July 1881. Only fourteen months later the first train on this line steamed into Ottawa. A bridge across the St. Lawrence was a major sticking point, however, and in 1885 a railway car ferry was installed at Couteau Landing to join the two sections of line to complete the route to Vermont. The 138 miles of railway, including the ferry had been financed primarily out of J.R. Booth's pockets. Booth and his colleagues petitioned the government in 1885 and 1886 for funding, but it was only after a direct appeal by Booth and Perley to the Prime Minister that they were given approximately $5,500 per mile. Finding money to finance his projects was not always easy, and was sometimes a considerable worry for Booth.

The bridge was still a problem. Some people were afraid that it would flood the surrounding area, others said it could not be built without blocking ships on the river, and others thought privately that the Grand Trunk Railway was lobbying against their competition. Booth approached Prime Minister John A. MacDonald once again, and was told something might be possible if a certain political candidate were to win the riding of Renfrew. Booth campaigned for the man at personal expense, the candidate won, and Booth was told within days that the government had approved the Coteau Bridge. Construction of the one and a half million dollar bridge began in May 1888, in great part due to Booth's "energy, influence and money" (Bell 1991). By that time negotiations for junctions with the Grand Trunk and Canadian Pacific Railways had been successful and the southern end of the Canada Atlantic line connected with three American rail lines. Thus Booth would have access to ice-free ports on the American Atlantic coast.

### The Ottawa, Arnprior and Parry Sound Railway

The line to Ottawa was not enough for Booth. As early as 1883 he had turned his attention to the lands west of Ottawa, in which lay the majority of his timber limits. The Canada Atlantic and Booth would have greater prosperity if there was increased transport of freight through Ottawa from the west, so Booth set out to accomplish just that. A railway crossing his limits would also afford a year round supply of logs for his mills, delivered at a cost savings as compared with those driven down river, with greater speed of delivery (Benidickson 2000). (So large and wide-spread were his holdings that such a railway would not cross all of his limits, so Booth would have to continue to drive logs down the tributaries of the Ottawa River.) But timber and lumber would not suffice to provide enough to make a profit, so Booth began to think about shipping grain from the prairies. If a railroad west could be built and the right ship connections made, there would be a good supply of business for the Canada Atlantic Railway.

It was J.R. Booth personally who conceived the 264-mile rail route westward from Ottawa, and it was Booth who financed much of its construction, with hard-won government subsidies at the municipal, provincial and federal levels. The new railway line would cut off 800 miles (1,287 km) from the traditional shipping route for grain through the Great Lakes from Chicago to Montreal (Coons 1978).

Booth chartered two railway companies in 1888, the Ottawa and Parry Sound Railway, and the Ottawa, Arnprior and Renfrew Railway, which were later amalgamated as the Ottawa, Arnprior and Parry Sound Railway in 1891 (Lavallee 1964). Author Don Beauprie writes that chartering two companies was a maneuver to gain government subsidies; subsidies for a line between Ottawa and Renfrew had previously been given to the Canadian Pacific Railway and would not be duplicated (Beauprie 2011).

While it seems strange at first that Booth would be permitted to build a railroad across Algonquin Park, newly formed in May of 1893, it is less the case when one considers that one reason the Park was created was to set aside a forest reserve. Lumbermen would continue to have access to their timber licenses and government rangers would be on patrol. Booth once suggested that for every tree he harvested, twenty were destroyed by fire (Coons 1978). Booth was not just thinking about immediate needs; he looked to the future and he believed in the forest industry. Booth predicted that *"if fires are kept out of the forests there will be more pine in this country 100 years from now than there was fifty years ago, and we shall have lots of timber for the generation to come"* (Anonymous 1906). So, the lumbermen played a role in the Park's establishment by not objecting to it. They would not be adversely affected by it, and they would have enhanced fire protection. As suggested in Algonquin Park's Track and Tower trail guide, *"you can be sure that there would not have been an Algonquin Park without Booth's agreement"* (Strickland 1992).

But Booth did have concerns. In *Algonquin Story* we read that *"J.R. Booth was not too pleased to find that his railway would run through the southern end of the proposed Park; and wrote a letter to the Department, suggesting forthrightly that the Commissioners' plans be changed to keep the Park clear of the Ottawa, Arnprior and Parry Sound Railway, whose line was already surveyed"* (Saunders 1946). That survey had been completed in April, 1892, just before Algonquin Park was established by the Ontario legislature. It is notable that Booth wanted the Park boundary moved, not his railway.

As with many of his grand schemes, Booth faced opposition to his railway plans. In 1892 and 1893, the Toronto business community was very much against Booth's railway and any financial subsidies Booth was getting, or might get, from government. It was argued that the east-west line across the Ottawa Huron Tract was unnecessary because the land had been found to be unsuitable for farming, and lacking in mineral wealth and population (MacKay 1981). There was also the concern that trade through Toronto would be diverted away by the new line. It was suggested that Booth's real purpose in building the line was to ship logs from his timber limits, and build his personal and business interests at the expense of the people. While Booth would indeed gain from the line, he fired back that he was developing the line for new business for Canada and to capture business that was currently travelling through American ports (Bell 1991).

Other railways continued to attempt to quash the competition. In particular, the Canadian Pacific Railway engaged in many disputes with Booth, and the two railways competed for construction workers. The CPR had announced that it intended to buy up the Parry Sound Colonization Railway, which would be needed by Booth to complete his route. But it was Booth who had the sympathy of the local inhabitants, and it was he who bought that railroad and gained access to Georgian Bay. There was an issue regarding a level crossing near Arnprior and a long court battle to win the route through the Hagarty Pass, near Wilno, where it was said there was space for just one rail line. Booth claimed that CPR surveys were trespassing on lands on which he had the right to build his railway. Booth won out in the end, in both cases (Bell 1991). While the court battle raged on, Booth's men continued the construction of the railway.

Road-bed construction had reached Barry's Bay and Madawaska by September, 1894 (Lavallee 1964). The building of the railway through the southern part of the Algonquin Park is a story in itself (well told in Don Beauprie's book, *Destination Algonquin Park*), for the route crossed through the Algonquin highlands. This was an area fully covered in forest. The rock was exceptionally hard. Temperatures in winter could reach minus forty degrees.

According to railway historian Niall MacKay, the right-of way through the agricultural lands from Ottawa through Renfrew and Arnprior and up to Golden Lake was fairly easy to construct. There were many embankments to build, and culverts to construct, and each mile required two miles of 72 pound rail and 2,800 ties with ten inches of ballast. The section leading to the Hagarty Pass near Wilno required the construction of *"a continuous climb of 425 feet in nine miles at an average of point nine percent grade."* The cost for this section of the line had been $153,466, including a subsidy of $33,600 (MacKay 1981).

The route of the section of the railway through the rolling hills of Algonquin Park, on which construction began in 1895, proved more expensive, as it required much more work to keep the grade within the limits of the engines that would run on the line. Numerous rock-cuts were blasted through the hard rock of the Canadian Shield. It was reported that one hundred and fifty tons of dynamite were allocated for construction in the summer of 1896 alone. Although many accidents happened all along the line, it is of interest here that a disastrous explosion in one rock-cut two miles west of Whitney killed three men, and injured another. A special train was sent to recover the bodies (Trinnell 1998). There were other accidents in the Algonquin Park area as well, among them the unfortunate case of one J. Potts who was injured when a heavy stone fell on his leg at Joe Lake. His leg was amputated below the knee. In another incident, a labourer fell between moving cars and was run over. Men had been loaded into crowded boxcars rather than coaches for transportation to work and the unfortunate man had tried to get to a flatcar where there was more room, and had fallen (Trinnell 1998).

*"The next 17-mile section was relatively easy to construct, as it roughly followed the shores of Long, Rock, and Whitefish lakes, ending up at Lake of Two Rivers. From Whitney it climbed at an average of 16 feet per mile for three miles, then continued almost level for the next fourteen miles, dropping only 28 feet in that distance."* In some sections, because of the difficulty in obtaining ballast nearby, a multitude of temporary trestles were built, to be back-filled when possible within two years; where bays of lakes had a rock bottom that would not accept pilings, rock-filled cribs were constructed to support trestles, two as long as 1,000 feet (MacKay 1981). Cyclists on the Old Railway Bike Trail between Rock Lake Campground and Cache Lake will have a sense of the route because it is on the old roadbed, now cleared, that they travel.

The Fauquier brothers had the construction contract (Trinnell 1998). The road bed was built with man-power and horse-power, using shovels and picks, wheelbarrows and horse-drawn scrapers. Where rock had to be removed after blasting, it would be hauled on carts running on wooden rails. Culverts had to be built, sometimes of laid stone, like the one that can be seen on the Madawaska River between Lake of Two Rivers and Pog Lake. Limestone was quarried and cut for bridge abutments and shipped by rail. Trestles were made of logs, some locally cut. Even where the path was easy, along the shorelines of lakes, embankments had to be made so the grade would be level. A labourer would be fortunate to make a dollar a day working at the construction of the railway.

The next difficult section ran from Lake of Two Rivers to Scotia, north of Huntsville, as it crossed a major divide of land. *"These 51 miles consumed 144,623 cubic yards of ballast, 142,576 ties and 4,563,786 board feet of timbers, which averaged 12 by 12 inches in cross-section. The total cost was $1,115,061.93 or an average of $21,808.00 per mile"* (MacKay 1981). That section required three steel bridges and a steel trestle 550 feet long and 76 feet high.

*"The greatest obstacle encountered was a ledge of granite 183 miles from Ottawa. The "summit cut" was 3,000 feet in length and required 5,000 pounds of dynamite to blow out rock 35 feet deep which would be used for fill in the valleys as a base for the railway tracks."* (Trinnell 1998). The line reached the Toronto-North Bay line at Scotia Junction in December, 1896, and was amalgamated with the Parry Sound Colonization Railway which allowed for the extension of the route from Scotia Junction to Depot Harbour (Lavallee 1964).

The area south of Parry Sound was also difficult as it required much bridging (Bell 1991). The section from Scotia to Parry Sound had been constructed, in part, in 1886, but then the Parry Sound Colonization Railway had run out of funds. This section, too, required great expense to construct. At Depot Harbour, the western terminus of the railway, *"the engineers found a natural harbor with a perfectly protected channel, deep enough for the largest steamships on the lakes, and three eighths of a mile in width"* (Anonymous 1897). However, even here, much work was required, including both the excavation of rock in some places and the addition of rock and soil in others (MacKay 1981).

A roundhouse and divisional point was built at Madawaska in 1896. It is not exactly clear why that location was chosen, but the proximity to Booth's Egan Estate limit cannot be coincidental. This did not please the populace of Barry's Bay, who filed a petition to the Minister of Railways, describing Madawaska as *"a place which is a complete wilderness wholly uninhabited and a considerable distance from any settled district."* They suggested that land could be obtained in Barry's Bay at reasonable cost, where the division point *"would be of immense benefit to the surrounding municipalities and to the country which aided in its construction"* (MacKay 1981). Madawaska became, for a while, an important maintenance point on the rail line. It was the site of a five-bay roundhouse (later expanded) and coal chute. Booth had a store and a post office there, as well as company offices and a boarding house.

Although Parry Sound remained part of the railway's name, Booth decided against a terminus at that harbour. When Booth bought into the Parry Sound Colonization Railway it was assumed by the local populace that they would soon see construction of grain elevators and an expansion of their town. Of course, landowners set a high price for their properties, expecting Booth to buy them up for the right-of-way and port facilities. It was not to be so. Booth found a better harbour on Parry Island, a few miles south of Parry Sound. Parry Island was an Indian Reserve, but Booth took advantage of legislation that permitted the forced purchase of Indian lands for railway construction (Gutsche and Bisaillon 1999). In 1899, Booth bought additional lands on the island and developed the entire shipping complex of Depot Harbour, including concrete docks, grain elevators, railway sidings and a round-house, and extensive freight sheds. A company town grew up around those facilities. December 21, 1896 was the official opening of the railway, although regular traffic did not begin until 1897.

The official amalgamation of the Ottawa, Arnprior and Parry Sound Railway with the Canada Atlantic to form the Canada Atlantic Railway took place in 1899 (Adamson 1939). Canada's Prime Minister, Wilfrid Laurier once called the Canada Atlantic Railway *"one of the most important which have been constructed of late years, probably the most important since the building of the Canadian Pacific Railway"* (Bell 1991). Governor-General Earl Grey commented that Booth had his personal admiration, since not only had he built a railway over 400 miles in length (half without government assistance) but he had built that rail line through a forested area without causing a forest fire or having one start because of a locomotive (Anonymous 1906).

### If you build it, you can move logs.

Shortly after Robert Phipps' visit to Lake Nipissing and Lake Nosbonsing, Booth again demonstrated that no obstacle was too big for him to overcome in securing logs for his mills. Some of those same dark pine forests, which he hoped to saw into lumber in Ottawa, lay around Lake Nipissing, the waters of which flow into Georgian Bay. Five miles away and over a height of land lay Lake Nosbonsing, a headwater of the Mattawa River flowing eastward into the Ottawa River. Rather than drive his logs from Lake Nipissing down the French River to Georgian Bay and then take them by ship and barge to Ottawa, Booth built five miles of railway line and engaged a barge to transport a full-sized steam locomotive and ten flat cars from the closest railway tracks, owned by the C.P.R., to his bush railway. The "J.R. Booth" pulled thousands of logs across the Nipissing and Nosbonsing Railway for many years. Those logs were driven downstream to Booth's Ottawa sawmills. It was certain novel features of the railway that prompted a write-up in the *Canada Lumberman,* in December, 1896, quoted here at length:

*"The terminus at Lake Nipissing is Wisawasa, where the creek of the same name empties into the lake but the bank is very steep, being 65 feet above the level of the lake. This creek was harnessed to draw the logs up to the top and load them onto the cars. A building was built into which the logs were carried to be loaded. The building is 220 feet long by 45 feet wide. The rear end is on a level with the ground, and the front end, supported by heavy framework, is 65 feet above the level of the lake. A jack ladder, 150 feet long, conveys the logs to the building by an endless chain, which is operated by a rope drive 500 feet long. A raised platform extends the full length of the building, and in the platform, or table, is an endless chain operated by another rope drive, 1,150 feet long. These rope drives derive their power from a water wheel 44 inches in diameter, under a heavy head of water passing down a flume of 6 X 8 feet. The water wheel, by means of a friction clutch, drives a fire pump when required, by which the railroad engine is supplied with water. An annex, 30 X 50 feet, covers the wheel and pump. The shafting is 3 7/8 inches in diameter and on this shaft are two grooved wheels around which the ropes rotate.*

*Alongside the platform are shunted four flat cars, with two birch stakes in each, against which the logs run from the table. Each car is 18 feet long, and is built of red oak lumber on tamarack bunks. As the jack ladder chain dumps eight logs per minute on the platform, the chain carries them along and they are dumped or slid onto the skids and then onto the cars. Seventeen men are required to do the loading.*

*When a car is loaded, a fork chain attached to one side binds the load on, being tightened by a ratchet wheel and dog. In the handling of the logs a great deal of bark is knocked off, which drops through the floor into a shute [sic], and is carried down into the lake.*

*The road is five miles in length, with two miles of sidings and switches; one switch extending to the Grand Trunk Railway. Twenty-two cars are taken each trip. Upon the return of the twenty-two empty cars, they are left on a siding. The engine then pulls out eleven cars already loaded to another siding, and eleven of the empty cars are run into the building, where they are quickly loaded. The engine then picks these up and with the other eleven the load is completed. At the terminus the track slightly declines toward the lake, the chains are let go and the logs glide off into the water. Two men are employed here to break up jams. Here the screw tug "Nosbonsing" tows the logs down to the Mattawa.*

*The rolling stock consists of 35 flat cars, which carry an average load of 19 logs. Thirty-three of these cars are in constant use, two being kept in reserve. They are 18 feet long by 10 feet wide, and are mounted on standard wheels and axles. The locomotive engine has been in use twelve years, and was built by the Rhode Island Locomotive works. A competent engineer and fireman are in charge, and four brakesmen are employed on the train. The road is level and everything runs smoothly. Four section men keep the road in good repair. The round trip has been made in one hour. It requires but two and a half minutes to dump the 22 car loads into Lake Nosbonsing. Ten loads a day are made, thus carrying over 4,000 logs.*

*The large steamer "Booth" of 100 tons, gathers up the logs around the shores and a smaller tug does the booming etc. There are two wharves at Wisawasa, and two men are constantly employed cutting up the flood wood which collects in the booms, for fuel for the boats. Six men feed the jackladder chain. Mr. Thomas Darling, the manager at Wisawasa, is a trustworthy man, and has been in Mr. Booth's employ for many years"* (Anonymous 1896).

The Nipissing and Nosbonsing Railway closed in 1912.

### A Lasting Impact on Algonquin Park

Not only did the Canada Atlantic Railway line make it easier to get logs to Ottawa but it also made it easier to deliver supplies to Booth's lumber camps. Where his camps were distant from the rails he built connecting tote roads. One such road ran from the rail line at Rainy (now Rain) Lake all the way up to the Nipissing River. The railroad also made it easier to get men into the camps. The late Joan Finnigan interviewed Larry Gaffney III about the role the railway played in the hiring of men into one of Booth's lumber camps:

*"Booth [the company] was always hiring and firing men. The men came in, in boxcars. They used to bring them off from the main line and into the Egan Estates. They'd come out of the boxcars and they'd line them up and out of thirty or forty they might pick half a dozen. If they'd had a man the year before, and he was a good man, then he was immediately hired. If they had quit early on them the year before, or if they had done anything out of line, there was no point in them being there. They would look to see if they had braces and, if they had, that was a good point; they weren't going to be hitching up their pants all the time. They looked to see if they smoked pipes – if they rolled their own cigarettes that took time out, too. Then they shipped them back again. They fed them – they always fed them – and then they would ship them back"* (Finnigan 2004).

In a few areas it was possible to carry logs from the forests, not only for his company but for others. No sooner was the line open than steam-operated sawmills sprang up along it, most notably at Canoe Lake (The Gilmour Lumber Company) and at Whitney (The St. Anthony Lumber Company). Even after the Grand Trunk Railway bought up the Canada Atlantic Railway in 1905, Booth continued to ship logs on the line.

Booth had his own mills to keep supplied with wood, and, as previously mentioned, the railway offered a means to keep the band saws at Ottawa, as well as hundreds of men, operating year-round, particularly in winter when mills were usually idle. To access one of his main timber limits, in 1899 Booth constructed a 20-mile (32-kilometre) spur line from the Egan Estate station, a short distance west of Madawaska, into the heart of the limits that had helped make his fortune. The McAuley Central Railway (sometimes called the Egan Estate Branch) extended past McCauley Lake and as far into Algonquin Park as the Head of Steel at Kitty Lake on the Opeongo River, just a few miles from Booth's namesake lake and close to the Booth Farm. Two small engines brought logs out to Madawaska where the cars of logs were transferred to the main line from the branch line. *"By this arrangement the time from the "stump to the saw" is reduced to 24 hours, whereas, by the lake and river routes it usually covers six months and in dry seasons even a year or more"* (Anonymous 1902a).

Another branch line running off the Canada Atlantic Railroad into Algonquin Park's forests was the Whitney and Opeongo Railway, which ran about fifteen miles from Sproule Bay, at the south end of the St. Anthony Lumber Company's Lake Opeongo limits, to Galeairy Lake and their sawmill at Whitney. Straight sections on the modern road from Highway 60 to Lake Opeongo reveal its earlier function as a rail bed. The *Eganville Leader* reported in 1902 that:

*"After fifteen months continuous labour the railway extending from Whitney Station on the western division of the Canada Atlantic to Lake Opeongo was completed last week. Lumber trains are now running on the new line, which connects the limits of the St. Anthony Lumber Company, bordering on Lake Opeongo, and the mill at Whitney. By construction of the railway, which is 15 miles in length, a saving of 50 miles is effected in the transportation of logs. Hitherto they have been moved to the mill by a round-about water route, which entailed a journey of many days duration. As this route was only accessible about seven months in the year the mill had to close down the rest of the time. With the transportation by rail the steam plant can be operated the year round if necessary.... The road connecting the St. Anthony Company's limits and mill is of the standard gauge size and was built with faithful observance to the ethics of good and permanent railway work. For the greater part of the route the railway passes through Ontario's natural reserve, Algonquin Park....The new road was constructed at a cost of $200,000, this high expenditure being made necessary by the large amount of rock cutting and trestles, each over 400 feet in length, and a great height....At present two trains a day are run over the road, each containing eight 34-foot flat cars built at the Canada Atlantic shops, Ottawa, for the business. Motive power is supplied by Canada Atlantic engines leased for the purpose"* (Anonymous 1902a).

As owner of the Canada Atlantic, J. R. Booth, took an inspection tour of the new branch line in April, 1903, even before the ballasting was completed and while a steam hoist for moving logs was being constructed at Sproule Bay on Lake Opeongo (Anonymous 1903).

Such an undertaking today would need an environmental assessment, but it was not until after the cross-Park rail line had been completed that Canada's foremost naturalist, John Macoun, visited the Park and noted its impact: *"The effects of the passage of the railway and the cutting of timber roads through the park were well illustrated by the introduction of species of plants that are found as weeds in the open spaces and around dwellings. These have been followed by a few species of birds and a number of butterflies, so that every year greater changes will be observed..."* (Macoun 1903).

Where previously the Park could only be accessed by canoe, passengers on the Canada Atlantic Railway were afforded a more rapid and comfortable way to get to Algonquin Park. Some, who were close friends of Booth or of railway officials, were sometimes transported in business car "99". Such was the case in 1903, when Ottawa architect Ernest Machado travelled in the company of Mr. E.J. Chamberlin, General Manager of the Canada Atlantic, to begin a multi-day canoe trip through the relatively new park (Clemson 2014). Machado drew a diagram of the business car in his diary of the trip. It included separate rooms for dining, sleeping, and viewing the countryside from comfortable lounge chairs, as well as two "water closets" for personal hygiene. It is thought that Booth's private car *"Opeongo"* was constructed on similar lines. It was Booth's habit to travel in *"Opeongo"* to visit his Madawaska timber limits for his annual vacation. What had taken three days of rough travel by buggy each way took but a comfortable five hours each way thanks to the railway.

Larry Gaffney III commented that *"all the luxurious private cars that pulled into the siding at Egan Estates was one of the wonders of growing up there as a boy. I remember one time being taken inside to see the interior of J.R. Booth's private car – all mahogany and velvet and brass — but generally they were completely off limits. Even people like Minor McAdam, the walking boss, didn't go near them when they were sitting on the siding. I can't remember them all, but besides Booth's there were private cars belonging to politicians, dignitaries, and wealthy men from Toronto, Montreal, the States, Hon. E.A. Dunlop, Frank Stock, Governor Smith...."* (Finnigan 2004).

When Booth's rail line was crossing Algonquin Park, the Park was not *"the average man's wilderness"* that it eventually became, but the destination of a few wealthy fishermen. Gradually, Algonquin Park became further opened up to visitors not interested in making a canoe voyage to get there. Local stations where passengers could board or get off the train were located all along the line, including stations at Whitney, Rock Lake, Lake of

Two Rivers, Cache Lake (known as Algonquin Park station), Canoe Lake, Joe Lake, Brulé Lake, and Rain Lake in Algonquin Park.

When Booth sold the Canada Atlantic Railway to the Grand Trunk Railway in 1905, the public was aware that the selling price was fourteen million dollars; what the public did not know was that over twenty million dollars had been expended in its construction and operation. (O'Leary 1925).

By the end of the first decade of the Twentieth Century, when the line was operated by the Grand Trunk Railway, a number of tourist hotels had been established on the line -- some operated by the railway itself — which attracted tourists willing and able to spend a few weeks enjoying the Algonquin air. Indeed some guests came to Algonquin Park specifically for their health. One of the lodges, Mowat Lodge, became a base of operations for the artist Tom Thomson, who introduced "the north" to the urbanites of southern Ontario through his vivid paintings of the Algonquin landscape. Today, an interpretive display at Cache Lake in Algonquin Park remembers the railway and the lodge era.

The railway continued to thrive through Booth's lifetime, but during the Great Depression of the 1930s the railway business was declining. Thoughts about construction of a new highway through Algonquin Park had been around for about ten years, but were once again considered. A trestle was found to be less than safe and was condemned. Canadian National Railways, which had operated the line since 1923, decided not to make repairs. When Highway 60 was constructed through the southern part of the Park as a depression relief project, from 1934 to 1936, the railway was doomed. The route of the railway influenced the route of the highway from Ottawa to Huntsville, as it was important to maintain communication with certain settlements. Rail traffic from the east continued as far as the McRae Lumber Company mill at Lake of Two Rivers until 1944, and rail traffic from the west to Cache Lake ended in 1959.

*Road-bed construction, O. A. and P.S. Railway. Algonquin Park Museum Archives 135*

*Rock-cut through Canadian Shield at Islet Lake. Algonquin Park Museum Archives 079*

*Wooden trestle at Islet Lake. Algonquin Park Museum Archives 143*

PA-009347

*Rail-bed between Lake of Two Rivers and Cache Lake. Library and Archives Canada PA-009347*

*Gilmour Lumber Company Mill at Canoe Lake in 1903. Algonquin Park Museum Archives 7108*

*Canada Atlantic Passenger Train. Library and Archives Canada PA-27296*

*The Locomotive Roundhouse at Madawaska. Algonquin Park Museum Archives 364*

*The Madawaska Coal Chute. Algonquin Park Museum Archives 5594*

*Nipissing and Nosbonsing Locomotive. North Bay Museum*

C-025966

*Canada Atlantic Railway Business Car Interior. Library and Archives Canada PA-25966*

*Top: Nipissing and Nosbonsing Railroad terminus. Mackey Collection. Bottom: Train with log cars on the McAuley Central Railway. Library and Archives Canada PA-120341*

PA-120341

*Top: Either car "99" or Booth's private car "Opeongo" on a siding at Rock Lake. Drummond Collection, used with permission. Bottom: Loading logs at the south end of Sproule Bay, Lake Opeongo. Algonquin Park Museum Archives 3298*

# J. R. Booth: The Industrialist

PA-008561

*Unloading one of Booth's steamers at the grain elevators at Depot Harbour. Library and Archives Canada*
*PA-008561*

THE NAME J.R. BOOTH easily conjures up associations with logging and railway building, but not so easily with industry and shipping of goods. Booth readily grasped the concept that railways required freight, and that his route to Parry Sound would provide more than a means to bring logs to his mills. Indeed, it was mills of another sort that would benefit; mills grinding grain.

Shortly after the completion of the Ottawa, Arnprior and Parry Sound Railway, in an uncharacteristic gesture, Booth granted an interview with newspaper editor P.D. Ross. Ross reported that Booth had said: *"I have built the Parry Sound road partly for my lumber business, but that won't do alone. I've got to have a good grain business from Depot Harbour to Boston to help. And there may be some difficulty getting grain cargoes from Duluth.*" When asked how he might overcome such difficulties, Booth responded, *"Why, if the shippers will not come my way, I will have to put some big boats on the lakes"* (Ross 1925). If competitors would not provide grain for his ships, Booth said he was prepared to extend his railway into the northwest, beyond the head of the lakes (Ross 1925).

### Shipping Grain

Booth formed the Canada Atlantic Transit Company, registering it in both Canada and the United States, in 1898. He also built grain storage facilities at Depot Harbour, Duluth, Milwaukee and at Couteau Landing. (Benidickson 2000). Eventually seven ships were operated by the Canada Atlantic Transit Company: S.S. Newond, S.S. Ottawa, S.S. George Orr, S.S. Kearsage, S.S. Arthur Orr, S.S. Canatco, and S.S. Delwarnic. Interestingly, there was no S.S. J.R. Booth, yet logging tugs, Alligators, and railway locomotives bore his name.

With the infrastructure in place to ship grain from the west, and with the new line cutting almost 800 miles off the ship route through Lake Erie and Lake Ontario to the Eastern Seaboard of the United States, the railway through Algonquin Park became one of Canada's busiest and most important. Booth's concerns about competition were allayed when other shipping companies took advantage of the shorter route provided by the railway.

By 1905, when Booth and his partners sold the Canada Atlantic Railway to the Grand Trunk Railway, the line continued to be used to ship grain from Depot Harbour. More than 20,000,000 bushels of western grain were being transported annually in an eastward direction, while 200,000 tons of flour and package freight from the eastern seaboard returned westward (Coons 1978).

Commodities which made their way through the warehouses and elevators at Depot Harbour included wheat, flour, and livestock feed, all unloaded by men with shovels and two-wheeled hand carts, twelve bags to a load. When unloading began these carts were wheeled up a gangplank to the storage platform, but by the time the ship was emptied the trip was

downhill (MacKay 1981). Of course, when loading manufactured and pro-
cessed goods heading westward the process (and incline) was reversed.

The original elevators were designed to hold about a million bushels of
grain, but expansions, the last of which occurred in 1907, extended that
capacity to two million. The two freight sheds, six hundred and seven hundred feet long respectively, were eighty feet wide and sixteen feet high.
They were built on filled land where once there was thirty feet of water. A
trestle 2,300 feet long provided access to the sheds, and there was an additional platform at which four steamers at a time could dock to unload.

During World War One, troop trains used the line, and men had to be
stationed at the wooden trestles and bridges to prevent sabotage. Grain
shipments increased in support of the war effort. In the winter of 1915, fifteen ships awaited unloading. As grain was removed from the elevators the
harbor ice was cut with ice saws to enable a ship to move to the dock for
unloading (MacKay 1981). When the shipping season was at its height, the
elevators and sheds were operated twelve to eighteen hours a day if ships
were in port. Packaged goods arrived in over one hundred and twenty-five
carloads per day. Between shipments west and shipments east, the single
track line through Algonquin Park must have been very busy indeed. It
may be this was the time in which it was said that a train passed by every
twenty minutes (some heading east, some heading west) (Saunders 1946).

### Booth's Expanding Empire

The cornerstone of Booth's empire was his group of sawmills in Ottawa,
but early on Booth began to expand his interests into the United States. He
bought land for storing and sorting lumber, and built barge docks at
Rouses Point, New York in 1868 (Trinnell 1998), built a planing mill and
sorting yard in Burlington, Vermont in 1875 (Coons 1978), and opened a
sales office, in Boston, Massachusetts in 1877 (Trinnell 1998). He also
opened a box factory in Burlington, utilizing materials produced by his
own American mill (Coons 1978).

Throughout his life Booth made technological improvements to his
sawmills. If better saws became available they were installed. To keep his
sawmill production going in two shifts, night and day, in 1910 he began
lighting his mills and lumberyard with electric light, run from his three tur-

bines at the Chaudiere Falls. *"Everywhere, even the booms were brilliantly lighted by electricity"* (Coons 1978).

So important were his Madawaska camps, and so innovative was Booth, that a telephone was installed in No. 1 camp, near Madawaska, so that he could communicate with manager Mr. W.G. McKay at any time (Anonymous 1905). Booth had telephones installed on his limits near Lake Nipissing as early as 1889 (Trinnell 1998).

Operations in the mills were dependent on inventory such as lumber wagons, carts, and sleighs. Rather than purchase these, Booth had them made by his own company wheelwrights. Also at the main mill was one of the largest blacksmith shops in the district, and an extensive machine shop where parts were made to repair the machines in the mills, or in the bush. There also was a company harness shop (Anonymous 1925b). Horses for the mills and bush operations were provided from his vast farm holdings about the Ottawa Valley countryside.

Although Booth's prosperity was still based in sawn lumber, by 1904, Booth was seeing the beginning of decline in the market for sawn lumber. So, in 1905 he established a pulp mill, soon followed a couple of years later by an adjoining paper mill. Booth's paper mill could produce 150 tons of newsprint each day. He also purchased the limits of the Montreal River Pulp Company, which afforded him the ability to cut both pine and pulpwood off the same lands. With these ventures, Booth joined E.B. Eddy in supplying the growing demand for newsprint in Canada, the United States and Britain. In addition, it provided Booth with a use of softwood logs he had formerly had to sell. It is not surprising, then, to note that in the year 1908 Booth set up a cardboard plant producing 60 tons per day (Coons 1978).

Booth was also involved in other businesses. He joined forces with Renfrew's Michael J. O'Brien in investing in the Dominion Nickel-Copper Company which was based in the Sudbury area. Those holdings, never developed by Booth and O'Brien, were later sold to the British American Nickel Corporation. Booth was also a member of the Board of Directors for Foster-Cobalt Mining in 1907 and Canada Cement beginning in 1909. The directorship of the latter made much sense as Booth apparently had a fondness for building in concrete. All his mills in the early 1900s were built of concrete. Fire was the lumberman's constant enemy. Booth's sawmills and stacked lumber had accidently burned down many times, in Ottawa and at Rouses Point. One can speculate that concrete structures might be somewhat more resistant to fire than wooden buildings, and a sound investment. According to author John Trinnell, it was said in the *Ottawa Evening Journal* of April 21, 1893 that *"all of J.R. Booth's plans take concrete form"* (Trinnell 1998).

*A grain-hauling ship, the Arthur Orr. Dave Thomas Collection*

# J. R. Booth: The Man

*J.R. Booth formal portrait. Library and Archives Canada PA-028001*

---

**ALTHOUGH HIS ACCOMPLISHMENTS ARE** easily listed, it is a more difficult task to try to get a sense of J.R. Booth as a man. Perhaps the most telling indicator of Booth's character is that he asked, apparently, that his personal papers be destroyed after his death. It is said by family members that in 1943 (when the Booth firm was sold to Garfield Weston) all the records of his company, and possibly many personal letters, were burned in steel drums (Trinnell 1998). Thus, few records of his business survive, which makes the task of characterizing the man all the more difficult. He seldom granted interviews, and left no personal recollections. Thus, one becomes very much dependent on the assessment of others, quotations of the day and what few documents have survived in the hands of others.

## Booth In Business

J.R. Booth was not impulsive, only making a new business move after much deliberation. Throughout his entire working life he preferred to make decisions on his own, preferring to avoid partnerships, although sometimes engaging in them out of necessity. It was paramount to Booth that his word was kept (Stevenson nd).

On one occasion Booth had a business conversation with Gordon Fleck, his grandson. He advised *"firstly never to work for anybody but himself and secondly never to trust an American"* (Stevenson nd). That conversation took place while Gordon was working for Booth and wanted a raise. When the raise was refused, Gordon quit and went to Vancouver. Years later, Booth asked him to rejoin the company, but Fleck refused at that time, repeating back to Booth the advice he had been given earlier about only working for himself. Apparently this amused Booth greatly, and he was fond of telling the story to friends and relatives.

J.R. Booth had an excellent memory for names and faces, but also for perceived wrong-doing. He was promised a bonus if he brought his railway into Ottawa, but it took longer than expected. The bonus was refused by City Council because it was after the agreed date. Booth built a small building to serve as a station. It was just a small shack, and city officials assumed that it would be replaced by a finer edifice, but Booth left it that way because of the way he had been treated (Jenkins 1922).

Thomas Patrick Murray, of Barry's Bay, was also a significant lumberman who lived to an advanced age. He recalled a potentially difficult experience with J.R. Booth. In 1909, John Omanique had purchased a sawmill and had assumed that a particular timber limit near Bark Lake went with it, since it had been used by the previous owners of the mill. When Murray partnered with Omanique they continued to use the limit. Tom Murray was eventually visited by a bush ranger for J.R. Booth, the rightful owner of the limit. It turned out that Omanique, and then Murray, had been trespassing for four years. Murray was told that Booth expected a visit from him at first opportunity to explain why he had trespassed. Tom Murray recalled that he had arrived *"at Booth's office about 10 o'clock in the morning. Booth arrived with no more than three dollars worth of clothes on his back. At first J.R. Booth was fighting mad. He said we had trespassed on his limits and that he would charge (Murray and Omanique) $5000 for what* *we had done."* Booth left for lunch, while Tom Murray stayed at his office. One of Booth's men said that Mr. Booth was always in a better mood after lunch. It turned out that Booth's bush ranger had checked out Tom Murray and had established that the trespass was an honest mistake and that Murray was a hardworking businessman just getting started. *"Booth returned from lunch and said he had changed his mind. He offered to sell his subsidiary company that owned and operated the licensed area..."* [to Murray and Omanique] on very reasonable terms for a good price. Tom Murray later described Booth as *"the greatest man I ever met."* (Murray 2002).

John Booth could be civic minded in his business relationships. When there was a problem with the water supply for the City of Ottawa in 1914, Booth assured local politicians that in the case of a fire, he would shut down his mills, thus giving the city access to 4,000,000 gallons of water (Trinnell 1998). However, he could be quite contrary with civic officials. According to one biographer: *"His most capricious legacy was a jog at the end of Elgin street... Elgin Street runs twenty blocks or so north to the national War Memorial. At its south end it turns awkwardly to the east, dips under an overpass round a crowded traffic circle then melts into the peaceful curve of the Driveway on the Rideau Canal. The jog east is the result of John R. Booth personally moving surveyor stakes a hundred yards out of the way of his switching yards and facing down city hall officials when there was some thought of objecting"* (French 1963).

Like the commander of an army, Booth preferred to look at the big picture and make plans which would be put in place by trusted employees under his direction. Perhaps the most significant trait that made J.R. Booth a successful business man was that *"a course once determined as right was irrevocable"* (Adamson 1939). It was said of him that his motivation was not in amassing large sums of money, but in the satisfaction of accomplishment.

Only in 1921 did he permit his holdings to be incorporated as J.R. Booth Limited, with himself and his children as directors. *"For seventy years the firm which now merges into the joint stock company has been conducted personally by J.R. Booth.... It has been said more than once that the firm of J.R. Booth has for some years now been the largest business in the entire world operated as the property of one man"* (Anonymous 1921). When it first was suggested that he should relinquish sole ownership of his holdings and become a company under the title J.R. Booth Limited, Booth objected, saying *"No! J.R. Booth was never limited"* (Stevenson nd).

### Booth as an Employer

J.R. Booth had a strong relationship with his workers. While the majority of his workforce was generally transient, seasonal, and unlikely to become involved in organized unions, labour issues did occur. During a strike over wages and working hours in 1891, Booth held firm and possibly supported the eventual intervention by the militia and police.

In 1918 there was a strike of pulp workers and boiler-men. Four hundred unionized men quit work over a demanded wage increase, and garnered support in some circles, but Booth refused to give any ground. He wrote a letter of protest: *"All the timber lands that I hold I bought in the open market in the same way P.D. Ross, editor of the Ottawa Journal, might buy a printing press, and I paid for most of them a price that was considered exorbitant at the time....I have not written this letter to boast of what I have done but I do not wish people to think that I have got something for nothing, and that I am unfair to my men with whom I have had the best relations for so many years, and shall have again, if outsiders would not seek to stir up strife"* (Trinnell 1998).

On another occasion, a strike was threatened within the Booth sawmills. There was to be no concession on that occasion. It was reported that Booth gathered the men of the mill about him and made a speech explaining his position. In essence he said: *"Boys, most of you have worked for me for a good many years. I have always tried to treat you fairly, and just as soon as I can see my way clear I intend to raise your pay. I do not owe a dollar on this mill and I will shut it up tight before I will let anybody drive me to pay wages the business will not warrant."* Booth's men knew their boss, and that he would not bluff when it came to matters of business. It likely took some persuasion of the leaders by the more conservative men, but the strike was averted (Anonymous 1925j).

It would appear that Booth's relationship with his men depended on the current fortunes of the lumber industry, and perhaps whether an idea was his or not. In 1895, when no strike loomed on the horizon, Booth modified the working day for the men in the mills from eleven hours to ten hours, and made no change to their daily pay (Anonymous 1925h). In 1911, he instituted an eight hour work day, without request by employees (Hugheson and Bond 1987).

Another incident, in which he cared more for his workers than the "bottom line," took place in the summer of 1910. Workers of the Grand Trunk Railway went on strike, causing a shutdown of not only transportation by rail but also the Booth mills that so depended on the railway. With the mills not running, more than 2,000 workmen, most with families (and some of them large) were prevented from working. With each passing day the feeling of gloom increased in the mill. Eventually the regular Booth pay day came around, and with it the expectation of meager earnings. *"The first man in the long queue of workers who stopped at the cashier's wicket, gave a gasp of surprise on opening his pay envelope. The next man uttered an exclamation of joy, and soon the army of workmen who came up with crest-fallen features wondering how two week's expenses were to be paid out of one week's wages, was changed into a happy crowd. Every envelope contained full pay for the week lay-off caused by the railway strike."* (Anonymous 1925j). The cost to the "company" to look after the men was about $12,000 (Trinnell 1998).

In the *Ottawa Journal*, of 9 December, 1925, we read: *"The story is told of a man in charge of a certain department of the mill one day discharging an old employee who at once proceeded to the office and demanded payment of the wages coming to him. The noise that he made attracted Mr. Booth's attention, and he investigated and questioned the old man as to why he was quitting. "It's time to quit when the boss says I am an old man and no good" was the old man's reply. Mr. Booth called the boss and requested an explanation. The boss was outspoken. "Why," he said, "this fellow has got so old and feeble he is not worth 50 cents a day." J.R. leveled those little eyes of his (which shone like two little stars) at the boss and remarked: "_____ _____ has worked for me more than 40 years and there was a time when his services were worth more than 50 cents a day, and he is going to stay right here in this mill and draw full pay just as long as I run it"* (Anonymous 1925j).

On another occasion, one of Booth's long-time bush employees became extremely ill with pneumonia. It was presumed he would not survive. As his family held vigil through the dark of night, there came a gentle knock on the door. It was J.R. Booth, equipped with supplies for rendering an old-fashioned remedy. In his youth, Booth had been quite interested in medicine. He had the man wrapped in red flannel, and at his insistence he sat by the man's bedside until his patient's condition began to improve (Anonymous 1925j).

Despite his compassion for the ill, Booth's record was not squeaky clean when it came to child labour issues. Of course, in rural areas it was not unusual for a boy to head to the woods in his early teenage years, but there were rules about working in the Ottawa mills. A Royal Commission on Capital and Labour called John R. Booth to give testimony in 1889; *"he admitted freely that boys under twelve worked in his mills, and he had paid no attention to a newly passed Factory Act prohibiting it"* (French 1963). The Commission interviewed employees as well as owners. One fourteen year old boy, who had started work in the mill at age twelve and a half, said he worked from six in the morning until twelve, when he had a little less than an hour for dinner, then worked from one until half-past six at night. On Saturdays he only worked until 6 p.m. He reported there were also boys of eleven working in the mill. He made about 60 cents a day (Anonymous 1889). Indeed, it was never Booth's habit to pay high wages, and for many years he held the firm conviction that no man who worked with his hands was worth more than $1.25 a day" (Stevenson nd).

### Booth's Management Style

References to Booth's management style provide a lexicon of hard-nosed character. He was described as dogmatic, self-opinionated, domineering, ruling with an iron hand, and *"autocratic in the extreme"* (Benidickson 2000). *"His mastery was unchallenged. His commands were final"* (Anonymous 1925j). He also provided *"a strange mixture of the autocratic temper and the democratic spirit"* (Stevenson nd).

It was widely agreed that if Booth wanted something done it had to be done the way he said it should be done (Jenkins, 1922). He was not very fond of initiative or creativity in his employees, but he did favour surrounding himself with men of *"energy and ability."* (Adamson 1939). He gave *"curt, incisive orders...which mill-men and yard men alike are quick to fulfill."*(Jenkins 1922).

Yet, despite his old-fashioned, even feudal, approach to management, Booth was a man who cared deeply about the welfare of his men, and of his own business. If work was not being done to his satisfaction Booth was quick to make that known, but more often as not he would do so by removing his own coat and demonstrating the right method to his employee. *"There was practically nothing about the plant that he could not do himself"* (Anonymous 1925c).

Although he ran a vast business empire, Booth was not one to avoid the common man, particularly in his camps or in the lumber mill. Indeed he had a preference for the humble folk who had to work hard for a living. He felt he could learn something from just about everyone with whom he talked (Stevenson nd).

Booth was very much a hands-on person. *"The close of many a day's work at the Chaudiere mills found Mr. Booth with sweat-moistened brow, begrimed hands and a toil-stained suit"* (Anonymous 1925i). On one occasion a person who did not know Booth personally came to the office to speak to him. The stranger was told he could find Booth somewhere out on the mill site. After much searching, the stranger spotted a small man mixing mortar in a pit, and asked him where he could find J.R. Booth. One can imagine the stranger's surprise when the workman announced that he was the man he was seeking (Anonymous 1925i).

A similar story is told that when the Canada Atlantic Railway terminal was brought closer to the centre of Ottawa, there was a purchase of an old dilapidated storehouse which was made to serve as a station for a time. He frequently could be found there, assisting his workers in making repairs. A distinguished resident of Ottawa once recalled that, while leaving a Canada Atlantic Railway passenger car with a crowd of other passengers, he saw the very owner of the railway nailing up some boards on the station building to make a repair he thought necessary (Stevenson nd).

He did not like to acknowledge that his age or physical condition had impaired his ability in any way (Stevenson nd). Such an attitude sometimes put him in peril. In June 1924, a fire near Booth's limits at Madawaska threatened the Victoria Lake hunting lodge of Booth's long time friend and business partner Edward Curtis Smith. The fire approached within 300 feet of the lodge, but despite his advanced years Booth insisted on directing the fire fighting. Fortunately, he was willing to be persuaded to move out of the immediate area of the fire, which burned for a week (Coons 1978).

*"He never asked his men to undertake a task that he would not face himself. This tendency for sharing risky jobs with his workingmen in and around the mills and yards at the Chaudiere, more than once resulted in serious injury"* (Anonymous 1925j). When he was 86, he found himself supervising the demolition of a storehouse damaged by fire. A large beam fell on him and broke his leg. One day, while working with his employees on a coffer dam, some of the timbers in the dam began to give way. Booth and most of the workers managed to gain secure ground, but not before the ladder he was on was swept away; one man was swept away by the flood. Unscathed, Booth remained to help the others find the body of the drowned man, then supervised the repair of the dam (Jenkins 1922).

In such cases his family sometimes tried to point out that such manual labour was quite undignified for a significant business executive. Booth would reply that, despite all his reasons to worry and become physically stressed, his brain was at rest when he worked with his hands. Indeed, Booth recommended that anyone who had tough decisions to make with his brain would find quicker and easier solutions to his problems if only he would take on some manual task (Stevenson nd).

### Booth's Personal Life

J.R. Booth was a quiet and extremely private man. According to biographer J.A. Stevenson, J.R. Booth was *"essentially a shy man, he was fond of his family, and the quietude of his home."* He also said, *"his personality was a closed book save to his family, his employees and a small circle of old intimate friends"* (Stevenson nd). That has made the writing of this aspect of his life most difficult to capture.

Little is known of J.R.Booth's relationship with his wife, except that she *"was his greatest helpmate."* It is said that in their early days in Ottawa she not only cared for his home most efficiently but also took several men in from the mill as boarders. Rosalinda, described as *"an unostentatious and charitable lady"* (French 1963), became ill with pneumonia in 1886, and passed away that year at age 57 (Trinnell 1998). She is named Rosalinda on her grave. According to one of his children, Booth was all business with little frivolity, but perhaps other researchers can find evidence to the contrary. Jackson Booth recalled that *"in his youth the most fun he had was hoop-rolling, mud-slinging, and balancing on a rolling log without caulked boots"* (French 1963).

Booth seldom granted interviews, particularly to the newspapers, although he read them on a daily basis. Other than that, he read little. It is said that during his early years he seldom slept more than four hours a night, and did much of his planning in bed (Anonymous 1925i). *"He was in the habit of using the hours of darkness as he lay in bed for the purpose of working out his plans and making calculations about his business problems and he was able to do so without impairing his strength because for most of his life he found four or five hours of sleep sufficient for his needs"* (Stevenson nd). Like many successful men, Booth was an early riser. In his younger days, about age sixty, he would rise by 5 a.m. and be at work at the mill with the rest of the workers at 6 a.m. (Stevenson nd). In later years, at ninety-six, he would arrive at the office somewhat later, at 9 a.m. (Anonymous 1923).

Although he was a giant in the lumber industry, J. R. Booth was anything but the physically robust super-man one might expect based on stories of his life (Anonymous 1925d). He stood only about five feet five inches tall. He had white hair and sported a full beard. Those who described him commented particularly on his steel blue eyes, ruddy complexion, and his square-set jaw and pressed lips. His nose was notable; Booth's Rock in Algonquin Park, a prominent rise which overlooks Rock Lake, was formerly called "Booth's Nose" by early lake residents. A magazine article, written when Booth was 95, described him as *"a sturdy figure, medium of stature, and slightly stooped, with a face framed in snow-white hair and beard that would remind you of chiseled granite"* (Jenkins 1922). *"Despite being able to afford the finest of foods, he ate little, for he suffered from almost constant indigestion"* (Stevenson nd).

Booth was a man of personal determination. When he was 35, Booth became quite ill and could barely eat. He was working eighteen hours a day and his doctor recommended a sea cruise or he would end up in the cemetery. Booth responded that he could not afford the cruise and he would not go to the cemetery. Instead, he gave up coffee, a favorite, and got better (Anonymous 1925d). One often hears about how difficult it is to give up smoking. Although he had smoked two cigars a day for many years, in

1913 a skin problem and the advice of his doctors made him decide to quit. He never smoked again (Trinnell 1998).

Booth was described as a plain-living man of simple personal tastes, who *"ignored conventional fashions in dress"* (Jenkins 1922), preferring instead the comfort in winter of a heavy woolen coat, warm mittens and a winter cap with ear flaps. He was often to be found simply dressed in workman's coveralls.

Financially, Booth did well for himself, with a fortune in the tens of millions of dollars. He spent little on himself, and was not beyond reminding his employees of the benefit of thrift. *"His abhorrence of waste was often manifested to him in practical fashion. On one occasion when he was supervising a party of French-Canadian workmen who were piling up lumber in one of his yards, he noticed one of the men divest himself of a pair of overalls and throw them away. They were in a badly tattered condition and seemed on the verge of permanent dissolution into a dozen separate pieces. But Booth, noting the man's action, went quietly over and picked up the overalls. Taking out his knife he carefully cut off all the buttons and returning said to his employee, "Louis, are these your overalls?" The reply came that they had been, but were no longer fit to wear. So Booth quietly handed him the severed buttons saying "Here, take these buttons along. You may need them some day to sew on another pair. At any rate they will come in handy and save you from buying others"* (Stevenson nd).

In 1916, Booth was negatively affected by the new — and "temporary" — income tax to help pay for World War One. At a starting rate of 4% for most people, the rate increased to 25 percent on incomes over $100,000. With an income substantially higher, Booth obviously paid significant taxes. For many years Booth had been Ottawa's largest taxpayer, and as a man careful with his money he always waited until the last day without penalty to pay (Anonymous 1925i).

Some people with Booth's financial resources might be inclined to travel the world. A few attempts were made to get Booth to vacation and "feel like a rich man" but they failed miserably. Booth's daughter once coaxed him into going on vacation to Atlantic City for two weeks. On the first day Booth stated that he had risen at 5 a.m., and by end of that day had seen everything he wanted to see, and intended to go home (Trinnell 1998). On another occasion he was persuaded to try his hand at fishing in the Ottawa River, but the sight of some of his logs washed up on a small island was too overpowering and he abandoned his pursuit of fish to retrieve them. (Stevenson nd).

For vacations in his style, Booth preferred just a change of scene. Each year he spent a month or two on his Madawaska timber limits (Trinnell 1998). According to the *Canada Lumberman* journal of October 15, 1923, *"he is acquainted with hundreds of employees in all kinds of work there and every year he looks forward to his holiday in the midst of old friends. He will make his headquarters in his private car and his staff includes a highly trained chef and two trained nurses. Although he is 96 years of age, Mr. Booth is in constant touch with the affairs of J.R. Booth Ltd."* (Anonymous 1923b). According to Ernie Montgomery *"The private coach would be parked at McAuley Junction and he would spend his days seeing what was being taken out and also check the quality of timber. He lived to be an old man and he worked right up until the end of his life"* (Montgomery 1992).

Although born in the Province of Quebec, J. R. Booth was not bilingual. He once said that his parents had been too poor to give him the advantage of any language other than his native tongue. That statement was uttered during a rare public speech in 1896, made at a political meeting in Hull (Trinnell 1998).

Booth was quick to contradict those who thought he was an American; he was a Canadian. Politically, Booth was a Conservative; he did not run for office — he said he was too busy — but worked behind the scenes with his influence. John A. Macdonald, Canada's first prime minister, was a frequent visitor at his home (French 1963). He argued strongly against Wilfrid Laurier's election campaign in favour of reciprocity with the United States, asking his workmen to vote Conservative and issuing a strong statement to the newspapers. He was more open in making his influence felt in directing the politics within the Canadian lumber industry. He was a member of the Ottawa Board of Trade for 68 years (Trinnell 1998). J.R. Booth joined in the founding of the Canadian Forestry Association, primarily over his concerns regarding fire. He was also one of those who organized the Upper Ottawa Improvement Company, which collectively handled all the logs that came down the Ottawa River.

Booth's personal hobby was the raising of flowers. He seldom passed up an opportunity to take in a horticultural show (Trinnell 1998). So much was his fondness for flowers that horticulturists at the Dominion Experimental Farm named a species of chrysanthemum in his honour. He was also Honourary President of the Canadian Patriotic Fund, and as a patron of clean manly sport he was a supporter of the Ottawa Rowing Club and the Ottawa Amateur Athletic Association. Although he furnished funds for an addition to St. Luke's Hospital, he was not one to give away money easily. Although his conviction was that the best way to help others is to give them opportunity to help themselves (Jenkins 1922), it was also said of him that he was *"a very charitable man, but no one but himself knows the extent of his bequests..."* (Anonymous 1904).

He had no great liking for social functions, and was generally very reserved in the presence of strangers. He seldom went to the theatre or other social functions, and took part in no fraternal societies or clubs, with the exception of his membership in the Rideau Club, *"in which he rarely set foot"* (Stevenson nd). Likewise, Booth had a few eccentricities in his manner. For many years, he resisted the pressure put upon him by his family to purchase an automobile. There were two reasons: Booth actually liked being driven behind a horse, preferring to go out in a buggy or cutter, depending on the season; and besides, he did not want David Beauchamp, his long-time coachman who was unlikely to be trainable as a chauffeur, to be out of a job (Stevenson nd). He eventually owned three automobiles.

One habit which made him somewhat conspicuous in the streets of Ottawa was his use of an umbrella when travelling in his buggy or cutter. The umbrella was quite large, and served in winter to shed rain or snow, and in summer to provide shelter from the sun's hot rays. But like the man who carried it, that large umbrella was not ordinary. It was constructed in such a manner that a piece of cloth could be removed from one section of it, with the subsequent *"substitution of a piece of transparent material made of mica to permit an inspection of everything worth seeing as he drove along"* (Stevenson nd).

### Some J.R. Booth Stories
During a particular period of personal "Booth interest," in the 1970s, when this writer picked up a few Booth stories, it was still as Audrey Saun-

ders had described it when she was doing research for her book *Algonquin Story:*

*"Wherever Park old-timers gather to "swap" stories of the old days, "J.R." is the central, almost legendary figure. They delight particularly in telling how the great lumber king used to arrive in his camps at all sorts of odd times to see how the boys were doing. He had learned his business the hard way by working in the mills and camps: and to the end of his days he loved to pick up an axe or a cant hook and demonstrate that he was still one of the boys at heart. To many men who worked in the Booth camps in the Park, the Old Man, wearing felt boots and a padded jacket and as unpretentious as any of his workmen, was a familiar and respected figure"* (Saunders 1946).

A story is told of a group of Toronto businessmen who were guided on a trip up the Ottawa River by an old lumberjack wearing a navy blue serge suit with a bright red necktie. He related how he had once worked with J.R. Booth making shingles: *"Mr. Booth he learn how to keep money. I learn to wear the fine suit; he have millions and millions and I have only the five-dol- laire bill in my pocket. But, he added, as he adjusted his festive necktie," I t'ink I learn somet'ings Mr. Booth do not; Mr. Booth nevaire learn to wear the fine suit and feel like a reech man"* (Jenkins 1922).

Rene Dubreuil, of Whitney, worked for Booth in a lumber camp. He recalled:

*"Well, blankets, you got your two double grey blankets when you went in there and when you went out, well, you handed them back in. You had no sheet, pillow, or pillow case. You had two blankets and then a tick or a mark, that was just you filled up with hay. It was your bed not theirs. I guess other times were worse because in my time we had iron beds. In for J.R. Booth they all had iron beds. You had an iron bed and a spring, but no mattress. So, I've seen worse, where they had no bed, where you've had to make a bed out of poles. But in for Booth, before my time I don't know, but in my time they had iron beds....Well the food it was no variety, but it was good. You know you had all the cakes, pies, meat and beans.... No, I never saw an egg or a piece of bacon in the bush; not in a lumber camp anyway"* (Dubreuil 1976)

A contrasting food related story has it that one day a man was at Booth's headquarters and asked why they had jam — or some other luxury — there but not in the camp in which he worked. Booth, who was present, had not known of the discrepancy and ordered that it be remedied immediately. Some have said that Booth was the first to add potatoes and other vegetables to the camp diet, but that is likely part of the Booth mythology. Potatoes were often grown on lumber company farms long before Booth's time.

Another story is told how Booth one day was interviewing men for the position of clerk. Before he was to interview the candidates, Booth dropped a few sheets of paper on the floor. Man after man came in to the office and stepped over the papers before sitting down. Booth just waved them away and said he had seen all he needed to see. Finally a candidate entered the room, who, as he went to take his seat, picked up the sheets of paper from the floor, straightened them out and placed them on the desk. Booth immediately said *"You are hired."* The man asked if he wanted to see his credentials. Booth said he had seen all the credentials he needed to see as he wanted a man with enough ambition to work for his job. (unknown source)

It has been mentioned that Booth seldom dressed any differently than the working man. One story tells of a young lad who was to report to Mr. Booth for clerical work. He took the train and sat beside an elderly bearded gentleman. When they both got off at the station, the young lad asked the older man where he could find J.R. Booth's office. The older man said the office was up the hill and the young lad suggested that the older should carry his bags up to the office and he would receive a whole 10 cents for his trouble. The older man carried the bags up to the office. The young lad instructed the older man to let J.R. Booth know that he had arrived, whereupon the old man walked behind the counter and said, *"I am J.R. Booth, and I want my ten cents. The next train leaves here in twenty minutes. You should be on it."* (unknown source)

Booth was not for any great display of personal wealth. It is said that on the occasion of an injury he went to an American facility for treatment. On arrival he signed in as J.R. Booth, timber-man. Presumably by his manner and dress it was assumed that he worked in a lumber camp, so the hospital administrators had adjusted the bill to an amount they thought the old man might be able to afford; a few hundred dollars. When he came to pay what he owed, Booth pulled out an immense roll of bills. It took some coaxing to get it out of Booth that he was not an employee at Booth Lumber Company, but the owner (Jenkins 1922).

Another story attributed to Booth has it that he took a ride in a horse and buggy usually taken by one of his sons. When he got out from the buggy he gave the driver a fifty cent tip. The driver had the courage, or audacity, to mention to J.R. Booth that he usually got a larger tip of a dollar from J.R.'s son. Booth replied in something along the lines, *"That is different. That boy has a rich father, but I am an orphan"* (French 1963).

A tale is told which demonstrates the respect given to him by his men. It seems that one day J.R. Booth went out for a walk in a wooded area unfamiliar to him and uncharacteristically he became lost. When he was overdue back at camp his men went looking for him. An old shantyman found him sitting on a log. Instead of making a big fuss, the shantyman sat down beside Booth and the two chatted for a while about the old days. Eventually the shantyman suggested that if Mr. Booth didn't mind, he had best head back to camp. Booth offered to keep him company on the walk back. Nothing more was said about the boss being lost (unknown source).

No doubt there are many other tales, long lost.

*J.R. Booth and Family c1871. Library and Archives Canada PA-033272 detail*

*J.R. Booth and his adult children, Fred, Gertrude and C. Jackson. Library and Archives Canada PA-033999 detail*

# J.R. Booth: His Final Days

*J. R. Booth (centre) and his sons, C. Jackson Booth (L ) and Fred Booth (R). Library and Archives Canada PA-120161 detail*

As JOHN RUDOLPHUS BOOTH aged, he took up residence with his son at 252 Metcalfe Street, in downtown Ottawa. A change in his health was noted in June, 1925. In September of 1925 Booth once again visited his Madawaska limits, staying in his private rail car. That was to be his last visit to his Madawaska limits, and his time there was abbreviated to only one week because he had developed a cold. Earlier in September also he had last visited the mills he had constructed at the Chaudiere Falls. In mid-November he was confined to his bed. He was alert, his mind was clear, and he was still discussing business with his sons until a few days before his death. Gradually he lapsed into semi-consciousness and "slipped away quietly." on December 8, 1925 at 98 years of age (Anonymous 1925j).

All of Ottawa had hoped Mr. Booth would see the centenary of his birth, but as his health failed his death became expected. Newspapers of the day were ready with multi-page reminiscences of his life and accomplishments. In large headlines, The *Ottawa Citizen* referred to him as a "veteran Ottawa Lumber King", as Ottawa's best known citizen, and as a genius for industry (Anonymous 1925f). The *Ottawa Journal* referred to him as the "Monarch of the Upper Ottawa," and the last of the old timber kings.

### A Humble Man Put To Rest
Booth's death would have been widely known, if only because the otherwise ceaseless whine of the saws in his Chaudiere mills became idle at midnight, and thereafter until the completion of his funeral. Workmen from the mills were gathered in sorrowful groups large and small. The day off work was considered more of a "holy day" than a holiday. Visitation was held at the Booth house on Metcalfe Street. On ceremonial occasions Booth would have a flag flown on a staff over the garage, and on that solemn day the flag was at half-staff.

The early morning of December 10, 1925, saw hundreds of long-time employees of the late lumber king gathered at his home on Metcalfe Street. They were there to accompany their former employer to the grave-side, an offer which the family was grateful to accept. As the casket was carried out of the residence during the mid-afternoon, there was silence among the waiting crowds. Despite the frosty day, all hats were removed in respect as the solid bronze casket passed through the streets.

The funeral of J. R. Booth at a small church in Ottawa was well attended, but it was the funeral of a simple man. There was *"no elaborate church service, no solemn ritual, no pall-bearers and not even funeral music"* (Stevenson nd). He was buried in Ottawa's Beechwood Cemetery, where a large stone monument marks the family plot.

The newspapers of the day were filled with words of tribute. The Hon. Arthur Meighen said of Booth that: *"The words of admiration and good will one hears from all who worked for and with him are a tribute as well to his character as to the eminence of his place among Canadians"* (Meighen 1925).

Looking back over his life there is no question the man from Waterloo, Quebec — who had arrived in Ottawa with but a few dollars in his pocket — had made something of himself. He had worked tirelessly to build what eventually became a vast and diverse empire under his sole ownership and control. (Anonymous 1921). He had sent both of his sons to Queen's University at Kingston. His estate was probated at 23 million dollars, but that was after he had given away substantial sums as gifts to members of his family (French 1963). He had overcome many obstacles. There had been fires many times, financial risks taken, and the hardships of cutting a railway through the rocks of the Canadian Shield. Personal losses could not be overcome, no matter how industrious he was: in addition to losing his wife, his daughter Frances died at age two, his daughter Augusta Adella at age six, his son Frank at fifteen months of age, and his daughter May Belle at age twenty-three.

J.R. Booth's lumber company persisted for a time, based at Tee Lake in the Lake Temagami area of Quebec. Booth Lumber Limited was formed in 1943 when J.R. Booth Limited was split up, and was later amalgamated with Universal Oil Products of Des Plaines, Illinois in 1971. The pulp and paper part went to E.B. Eddy.

Some wondered why J.R. Booth had not been granted a knighthood. He had certainly accomplished a great deal. However, business disputes with Ottawa City Council regarding railway level crossings, use of piling yards, rights-of-way, and so on, as well as the necessity of federal court action to stop him from fouling the Ottawa River with sawdust, may have provided cause for concern regarding the granting of such a distinction.

Others thought Booth should be recognized as one of the Fathers of Canada. The *Ottawa Journal* agreed with Sir Arthur Currie that *"many of the facts concerning such great Canadian pioneers as Mr. J.R. Booth might very properly be incorporated in our school text books to impress the youth of*

*our country with the fact that the wealth accumulated today by certain indi-
viduals is not merely a matter of good fortune, but rather the willingness to
endure privations, the desire to work, and the character to stand up under
reverses"* (Anonymous 1925d)

Booth historian Clarence Coons stated that *"His vision, unerring judg-
ment, quiet manner, genuine sincerity and honesty all contributed to the
endurance of his position amongst Canadians" (Coons 1978).* With that
thought we close one of the great chapters in Canadian history, of which it
is worthwhile on many levels to know "more about."

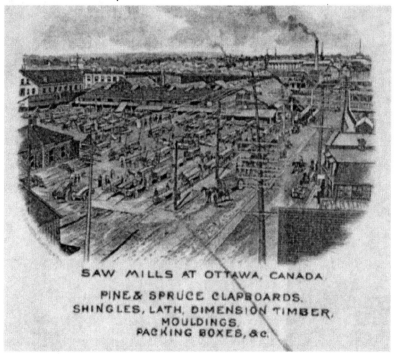

*Booth Company Letterhead c1890s. Smith Collection, University of Vermont Library*

*Booth Monument in Ottawa's Beechwood Cemetery. R. MacKay collection*

# Oh, One Last Thing

*Original Fleck House on Rock Lake c1920s. Drummond Collection. Used with permission.*

## The Barclay Estate

There were two properties in Algonquin Park that often have been thought or said to have a direct connection with J.R. Booth, but in fact do so only by family connection. Having little information on each we cannot provide much "more about," but perhaps can provide a "less on" about each.

The Barclay Estate on Rock Lake, now part of the Booth's Rock Trail in the Highway 60 region of Algonquin Park, was once a private residence. It was a grand estate in the formal sense if you will; a multi-level structure, with stone stairs leading to extensive gardens and manicured lawns. The residence was named Men-Wah-Tay, apparently meaning "Place of Sunshine". With a care-taker's house, boathouse with dance floor and games room above, ice-house, stable and blacksmith shop, extensive docks, and both a private railway siding and private station, it was an impressive summer home to say the least.

Some sources have attributed purchase of the land from the St. Anthony Lumber Company, perhaps by J. R. Booth, with inclusion in the 1897 sale of up to 5,000 acres of land. According to one source more than half of the original property was sold back to the St. Anthony Lumber Company in 1903. Nightingale Township records indicate that it was Andrew Walker Fleck, J.R. Booth's daughter Gertrude's husband, who purchased the land from the Crown in 1897 and patented it by 1905. Andrew Fleck was an iron-goods manufacturer in Ottawa who later became one of the managers of Booth's railways. The rectangular block of land included 7,000 acres. When the water area is removed, as well as the land set aside for the Ottawa Arnprior and Parry Sound Railway right-of-way up the east side of Rock Lake and land for a station at the head of the lake, what remained was about 5,000 acres of land almost completely surrounding Rock Lake. All but twelve lots were sold back to the Crown in 1909, before Algonquin Park expanded to include much of Nightingale Township in 1911.

Mr. Fleck arranged for the construction of a large house on a point jutting into the lake on the eastern side, on Lot 14 Concession XI, adjacent to the railway. The Flecks had four children, Gordon, Bryce, Rose and Jean, represented in name by Gordon Lake and the two islands in Rock Lake, Jean and Rose.

After Andrew Fleck died in 1924, the property was soon mortgaged by his widow, Helen Gertrude Fleck, through the Royal Trust Company. In 1934 the property passed to Gertrude Jean Barclay, Gertrude Fleck's daughter. She was the wife of Judge Gregor Barclay, a prominent member of Montreal society. Together they renovated the house built on this site. Each spring Mr. Barclay sent up from Seneville, Quebec many flowering plants; day-lilies, lilacs, Norway spruce, geraniums, and sylvias to beautify his summer home. Some years, Judge Barclay and his family spent July and August there; in alternating years he spent September as well. They would take an excursion two or three times a summer, along the trail kept clear for them, up to the top of Booth's Rock to take in the view. Visitors included Mrs. Barclay's brother Gordon, an avid fishermen, and friends from Toronto, Ottawa and Montreal. It appears that by that time the holding of land had been reduced to about 780 acres.

Some of the guests no doubt engaged the Barclays in a tennis match or two, played on the hard-surfaced tennis court. Chipped stone had been shipped up by train, laid down by hand and then rolled flat and compact with a large garden roller filled with water, and then surfaced with tar. According to former caretaker George Pearson, *"we rolled that and rolled that and rolled that."* The tennis court in the woods was, and still is, a sight to behold.

Some food might have come from a large vegetable garden near Gordon Lake, tended by caretaker Billy Baulke, but most supplies came by train. Groceries were dropped off by special arrangement near the estate and then transported the next 500 metres or so in by a stone boat drawn by a single horse. Fine furnishings, tennis, taking in summer breezes on the outside balcony; it must have seemed an idyllic life.

Located on the very edge of Algonquin Park in the early days of its existence, the property was simply a private residence in Haliburton County. When Nightingale Township (and adjacent Lawrence Township) became part of Algonquin Park in 1911 it had remained as a parcel of patented land. According to the Registry Office records, lot 14 and 15 remained in the ownership of Jean Barclay until the early 1950s. Her children, Ian Barclay and his sister Joan Drummond were very attached to the property, but by that time the difficulty and expense of upkeep was becoming great. The property reverted to the Crown in October 1953. Although it was not until 1954 that the government policy on leased and patented land within Algonquin Park changed, it must have been known that the property would have been selected to revert to the Crown at any rate. It is said that the house was last occupied in 1955, and it was dismantled by the Department of Lands and Forests in 1957. The railway right of way was given up by the Canadian National Railway Company (distant successor to the O. A. and P. S. Railway) in 1958. The reader interested in more photographs, is referred to *Rock Lake Station: Settlement Stories Since 1896*, by Gaye Clemson.

### The Turtle Fishing Club
The other building in Algonquin Park with an indirect connection to J.R. Booth was The Turtle Fishing Club on Lake Travers in the northern

section of the Park. Construction of this building on a two acre lease began in 1933 with the felling of 300 Jack pine logs, cut locally.

C. Jackson Booth, son of J.R. Booth, was part of a group of associates providing financing for re-developing Lake Traverse Lodge, a summer resort which had been opened in the late 1920s (MacDougall 1933). It was but a "stone's throw" from The Turtle Fishing Club.

Construction of the new building was recalled by one of the carpenters, in a 1976 article in The *Pembroke Observer*. Bill Fiebig said: *"We started in June and we were being paid $10 a month with board. We worked 10 hours a day, six days a week. Our job was to shape the logs with gouges and axes"* (Woermke 2009). He was one of seven Swedes, Finns, and an Austrian foreman, who laid the 35-foot logs so carefully no chinking was needed between. It is said the log work was done by the same skilled axe-men who built the very fashionable Seigniery Club, in Montobello, Quebec.

The layout of the building, when seen from above, formed the shape of a turtle, the bark mark of the late J.R. Booth and then Booth Lumber Company Ltd, of which Jackson Booth was a Director. A dining room twenty feet by thirty feet formed the body, along with the kitchen. Joined to the dining room were four bedrooms, each twenty-four feet by sixteen feet, each with a walk in closet and fireplace.

Apparently, for a time, guests of the Turtle Club were picked up from Lake Traverse Station in a Rolls Royce automobile that had been brought in to the site by train. Alas, the narrow and stump-ridden road to the camp took its toll, and the transportation of guests had to revert to conveyance by horse-drawn wagon.

After the death of Jackson Booth, the lease was transferred a number of times. Eventually the building fell into disrepair, and the lease reverted to the Crown. At the time of the Algonquin Park Master Plan the structure was designated as a historic zone. However, the building was dismantled with government permission in 1978, with the intention that it would be reconstructed elsewhere. Unfortunately, it was not. Now only the chimneys remain to mark the site of a most interesting piece of Algonquin Park architecture.

*Barclay Estate as seen from Rock Lake. Drummond Collection. Used with permission.*

*Barclay Estate Boathouse. The remains of the concrete piers can be seen today. Drummond Collection. Used with permission.*

*The Barclay Estate tennis courts. Drummond Collection. Used with permission.*

*The Barclay Estate lawn. Drummond Collection. Used with permission.*

*Train arriving at Men-Wah-Tay Station. Drummond Collection. Used with permission.*

*The Turtle Fishing Club from the air. Algonquin Park Museum Archives*

*The Turtle Fishing Club log corners. Algonquin Park Museum Archives*

*Turtle Fishing Club on Lake Travers in Algonquin Park. Algonquin Park Museum Archives*

*Remains of the Turtle Fishing Club chimneys that anchored each building wing. Algonquin Park Visitor Centre slide collection*

# References / Bibliography

Adamson, David, 1939. J.R Booth and the Canada Atlantic, *Canadian National Magazine*, May 1939

Anonymous, 1889. *Royal Commission on the Relations of Labour and Capital: evidence Ontario*, Ottawa

Anonymous, 1896. J.R. Booth's Logging Railway, *Canada Lumberman*, Vol 17, No 12, C.H. Mortimer

Anonymous, 1897. The Parry Sound Railway, in The Wood Industries of Canada, *Timber Trade Journal*, London

Anonymous, 1900. An Act to Amend the Algonquin National Park Act, 63 Victoria

Anonymous, 1902a. Lumber Railway Branch constructed to save 50 miles and greatly facilitate transportation, from November 26, 1902 issue, *Eganville Leader*, 75th Anniversary Souvenir Edition, 1977

Anonymous, 1902b. *Rod and Gun in Canada*, Vol 4 No 3

Anonymous, 1903. Article from April 15, 1903, *Eganville Leader*,75th Anniversary Souvenir Edition, 1977

Anonymous, 1904. Canada's Foremost Lumberman, *American Lumberman* Vol 1536

Anonymous, 1905. The Lumber Camps in the Upper Ottawa Valley, *Canada Lumberman*, Vol 25 No 5, May 1905, C.H.Mortimer

Anonymous, 1906. *Report of the Canadian Forestry Commission*, Ottawa, January 10, 11, 12, 1906, Government Printing Bureau

Anonymous, 1912. An Act to confirm certain agreements respecting the limits of J.R. Booth in Algonquin Park, 3-4 Geo V

Anonymous, 1921. Largest Business in World Owned By One Man, *Canada Lumberman*, Vol 41 No 3, Feb 1, 1921

Anonymous, 1923a. John R. Booth, *Christian Science Monitor*, March 19, 1923

Anonymous, 1923b. Mr. Booth on His Annual Holiday, *Canada Lumberman*, Vol 43 No 21, Oct 15, 1923, C.H. Mortimer

Anonymous, 1923c. Canada Atlantic Railway Co., typewritten report, Algonquin Park Museum Reprint #1888

Anonymous, 1925a. Mr. Booth Makes Big Shipment of Square Timber, *Canada Lumberman*, Vol 45 No 7, April 1, 1925, C.H. Mortimer

Anonymous, 1925b. Booth Co. Builds all of Accessories, *Ottawa Journal*, June 13, 1925

Anonymous, 1925c. The Boss Knows How Job Should Be Done, *Ottawa Journal*, June 13, 1925

Anonymous, 1925d. Industrial Achievements Based on Energy and Confidence, *Ottawa Journal*, June 13, 1925

Anonymous, 1925e. *Ottawa Journal*, Dec. 8, 1925

Anonymous, 1925f. Passing Occurs of Veteran Ottawa Lumber King, *Ottawa Citizen*, December 8, 1925

Anonymous, 1925g. Pioneer of Industrial Realm in the Dominion passes, his labour done, *Ottawa Journal*, 9 December, 1925

Anonymous, 1925h. Romantic Career of John Rudolphus Booth, *Ottawa Citizen*, 9 December, 1925

Anonymous, 1925i. Canada's Lumber King and Notable Figure in Industry Died Yesterday Afternoon, *Ottawa Journal*, 9 December, 1925

Anonymous, 1925j. John R. Booth's Death Closes Rich Chapter in Canada's Life, *Ottawa Journal*, December 9

Anonymous, 1977. *A Pictorial History of Algonquin Park*, Ministry of Natural Resources,

Beauprie, D., 2011. *Destination Algonquin Park*, General Store Publishing House, Burnstown

Bell, A., 1991. *A Way To The West: A Canadian Railway Legend*, Private Printing, Barrie, Ontario, 188 pp

Benidickson, J., 2000. John Rudolphus Booth, in *Dictionary of Canadian Biography*, University of Toronto

Brault, Lucien, 1946. *Ottawa Old and New*, Ottawa Historical Information Institute

Clemson, Gaye I., 2005. *Rock Lake Station: Settlement Stories Since 1896*, Trafford Publishing

Clemson, Gaye I., 2006. *Treasuring Algonquin: Sharing Scenes from 100 years of Leaseholding*, Trafford Publishing

Clemson, Gaye I., 2014. *Canoe Tripping in Algonquin Park: Then and Now*, Fast Pencil Publishing

Coons, C., 1978. "The John R. Booth Story", *Your Forests*, Volume 11, Number 2,

Cross, L.D., 2004, *Ottawa Titans: Fortune and Fame in the Early Days of Canada's Capital*, Altitude Publishing,

Dubreuil R., 1976. Interview of Rene Dubreuil by Ron Pittaway, Algonquin Park Museum Archives

Finnigan, J., 2004. *Life Along the Opeongo Line: The Story of a Canadian Colonization Road*, Penumbra Press

French, Doris, 1963. The Booths of Ottawa, *Chatelaine*, December

Gard, A., 1904. *The Hub and Spokes or The Capital and its environs*, Emmerson Press, Ottawa,

Gutsche, A. and C. Bisaillon, 1999. *Mysterious Islands: The Forgotten Tales of the Great Lakes*, Lynx Images

Hughson, J.W., and C. C. J. Bond, 1987. *Hurling Down The Pine; the story of the Wright, Gilmour and Hughson families, timber and lumber manufacturers for the Hull and Ottawa region and on the Gatineau River, 1800-1920*, Old Chelsea

Jenkins, C. 1922. J.R. Booth – On the Job at 95, *MacLean's Magazine*, May 15, 1922

Lavallee O., 1964. Ottawa Arnprior and Parry Sound Railway, *Canadian Rail*, number 156, June

Lambert, R. and P. Pross, 1967. *Renewing Nature's Wealth, A Centennial History of the Public Management of Lands, Forests & Wildlife in Ontario 1763-1967*, Department of Lands and Forests, Toronto

Lee, D., 2006. *Lumberkings & Shantymen: Logging And Lumbering In The Ottawa Valley*, James Lorimer and Company, Toronto

Lee-whiting, B., 1970. The Pointer Boat, *Canadian Geographic Journal*, Vol LXXX No 2

Lower, A.R.M., 1973. *Great Britain's Woodyard: British America and the Timber Trade, 1763-1867*, McGill-Queen's University Press

MacDougall, F.A., 1933, Letter to W.C. Cain, May 12, 1933, Algonquin Park Museum Archives

MacKay, N., 1981. *Over the Hills To Georgian Bay*, Boston Mills Press, Erin

MacKay, R., 2002. *A Chronology of Algonquin Park History*, The Friends of Algonquin Park, Whitney

MacKay, R., and Reynolds, W., 1993. *Algonquin*, Boston Mills Press/ Stoddart Publishing, Erin

Macoun, J., 1903, in Garland, G. 1989. *Glimpses of Algonquin: Thirty Personal Impressions From Earliest Times To The Present*, The Friends of Algonquin Park, Whitney

Meighen, A., 1925, Services of Nation Building Character, *Ottawa Journal*, Dec. 9, 1925

Montgomery, E., 1992. Interview of Ernie Montgomery by Don Stand-field, Silent Thunder Productions, transcript on file at Algonquin Park Museum Archives, Algonquin Park Visitor Centre

Murray, T., 2002. *The Sawdust Gene: Murray Brothers Lumber Company 1902-2002*, Murray Brothers, Barry's Bay

O'Leary, M.G., 1925. A Challenge to Youth, *Ottawa Journal*, June 13, 1925

Phipps, R., 1885. The Watershed of Eastern Ontario, Report of Clerk of Forestry, Sessional Papers (no. 4) 48 Victoria

Roberts, C.G.D., and A. Tunnell. 1934. *The Standard Dictionary of Canadian Biography; The Canadian Who Was Who*, Trans-Canada Press, Toronto

Ross, P.D., 1925. Mr. Booth's Supreme Courage, *Ottawa Journal*, Dec., 9, 1925

Saunders, A., 1946. *Algonquin Story*, Department of Lands and Forests, Toronto

Soucie, Alan, 2008. *Echoes of the Forest: Canada's Lumbering Story from Past to Present, Baico Publishing*, Ottawa

Stevenson, J.A., no date. Draft of Biography of J.R. Booth, Queen's University Archives, Kingston

Strickland, R.D., 1994. *Booth's Rock Trail: Man and the Algonquin Environment*, The Friends of Algonquin Park, Whitney

Strickland, R.D., 1992. *Track and Tower Trail: A Look Into Algonquin's Past*, The Friends of Algonquin Park, Whitney

Strickland, R. D., 1993. *The Best of the Raven*, The Friends of Algonquin Park, Whitney

Strickland, R.D., 2014. *The Best of the Raven, Vol. 2*, The Friends of Algonquin Park, Whitney

Trinnell, J. R., 1998. The *Life And Times Of J.R. Booth*, TreeHouse Publishing, Ottawa

Westhouse, B., 1995. *Whitney: St. Anthony's Mill Town On Booth's Railway*, The Friends of Algonquin Park, Whitney

Woermke, G., 2009. *Lake Traverse Station*, Private Printing, Ottawa

# About the Author

Roderick (Rory) MacKay is one of a number of Algonquin Park historians and Algonquin Park authors. He is a retired secondary school teacher of environmental science and Canadian history, and a former seasonal Interpretive Naturalist at the Algonquin Park Museum (1972-1978, 2000). His contributions have been recognized through receipt of the Directors' Awards of both The Friends of Algonquin Park and the Friends of Bonnechere Parks.

In 1993 he and photographer William Reynolds commemorated the centennial of Algonquin Park with their book *Algonquin*, which combined images of the landscape with a history of the Park. In 1996 Rory and The Friends of Bonnechere Parks produced a detailed watershed history, *Spirits of the Little Bonnechere: A History of Exploration, Logging, and Settlement, 1800 to 1920*.

The Friends of Algonquin Park and Rory have published: *A Chronology of Algonquin Park History*, an inexpensive overview of the events that have shaped Algonquin Park and their dates; and *More about the Algonquin Logging Museum Blacksmith Shop*, an inexpensive but detailed explanation of the equipment to be found in a blacksmith shop of the 1920s and the means by which the smith worked metal bars into useful things.

# Index

# Other Algonquin Park Heritage Publications

OTHER PUBLICATIONS ABOUT THE human history of Algonquin Park by Gaye I. Clemson include:

- **Canoe Tripping in Algonquin: Then and Now (2014)** -Compares canoe tripping experiences in September 1903 with the same trip taken over 110 years later with two women's attempt in the summer of 2013 to race from Canoe Lake to Cedar Lake and back in less than 20 hours.
- **Algonquin Voices: Selected Stories of Canoe Lake Women (2002)** - This narrative brings to life the lives of a number of women who lives artist Tom Thomson touched, during his time in the Park from 1914 - 1917 and many other courageous women who have lived and loved since 1905 on the shores of Algonquin Park's famous Canoe Lake.
- **Rock Lake Station: Settlement Stories Since 1896 (2005)** - For 40+ years one of the key stops along the Ottawa, Arnprior and Parry Sound railway was <u>Rock Lake Station.</u> For those camping enthusiasts, lease-holders and railway workers who settled on or visited Rock and White-fish Lakes in the early part of the 20<sup>th</sup>C the train was the lifeblood of this little community. This story shares the history of the coming and going of the railway and the surrounding settlement.
- **Treasuring Algonquin: Sharing Scenes of 100 Years of Leaseholding (2006)** - Among the many who treasure Algonquin Park are a small group of leasehold residents who have occupied small corners of the Park since the earliest days of the 20th century. Using current and historical narratives along with extensive research through files seldom searched, this narrative reveals the depth and breadth of their roots in the community and provides a glimpse into their lives, traditions and contributions to the Park's well being.

MORE ABOUT SERIES:

- **Gertrude Baskerville - The Lady of Algonquin Park (1st Edition 2001, 2nd Edition 2011)** - In the spring of 1941, Gertrude Baskerville set our from the Kitchener area with her ailing husband and teenage son to join her brother in establishing a new life on the shores of South Tea Lake. Within a year her husband had died, her son was shipped overseas, and her brother decided that better opportunity lay for him and his family in British Columbia. This is the story of the 'Lady of Algonquin Park' who carved out for herself a life in the wilderness for over 35 years.

- **The Ghosts of Canoe Lake: A Paddler's Guide to the Spirits of Its Lost Landmarks** (2010) - Most visitors to Canoe Lake are unaware of the history of the lake around them. This booklet is a paddler's guide to various points of interest. It is designed to identify locations, historical roots and to share stories about the human history of this unique locale.

- **Algonquin Park's Portage Store: The History of a Canoe Lake Institution** (2010) -Every week from early May to Thanksgiving in October, hundreds of visitors venture to Canoe Lake and visit the Portage Store be they day visitors out for an afternoon paddle, car campers, interior canoe trippers, or those just casually driving by along Highway 60. This booklet shares the rich history of this venerable institution since its original opening in the mid 1930's.

- **Nominigan and other Smoke Lake Jewels (2012)** - This narrative shares the stories of three important Smoke Lake voices including are the Northways who purchased and restored Camp Nominigan from the Grand Trunk Railway in 1931, Manley Sessions and his family, who tried valiantly to resurrect Minnesing Lodge on Burnt Island Lake in the 1950s and J. R. Dymond the father of the Park's Naturalist Interpretive Programs.

For more information check our web site www.algonquinparkheritage.com

CPSIA information can be obtained
at www.ICGtesting.com
Printed in the USA
FFOW05n1955040517

9 781619 336131